When Easter Interrupts

Dave and Dottie,

With so much love and appreciation
for you both in my heart, I wish you
the deepest joy of this Easter
season!

Much love
Budd Friend-Jones
February 22, 2010

When Easter Interrupts

Reflections on the Meanings of Lent and Easter

Gilbert Friend-Jones

FIRST EDITION

Cover photograph and design: WEG Thomas

ISBN 1450515142

Printed in the United States of America

*To my wife, Gretchen
whose unfailing support over the years of our life together
enabled these sermons to be composed,*

*and to my sister, Bonnie
whose life is a model of Easter hopefulness.*

Contents

Preface

Without a doubt, Easter presents one of the central koans of Christian spirituality. Its meaning cannot be fathomed by rational thinking alone, yet the intellect cries out to understand it. To affirm resurrection presents staggering challenges to those with contemporary scientific sensibilities. To ignore it makes a mockery of the essence of our faith. Thus we circle it. We study it, meditate upon and savor it, but Easter refuses to yield a singular meaning. We bring a post-modern consciousness to pre-modern narratives. For Easter to yield its truth to us, we must dwell for a time at the intersection of myth and history. We must look within ourselves as well as our texts. Easter defines the life of Christian faithfulness, but it always will be more premise than conclusion, more a framework for living than an explanation of life.

The reader will quickly discover that I am not a literalist, yet I try to be faithful to the texts. In so doing, I claim as my own these words from an Anishinaabe storyteller: "The story I am about to tell is true. It may not have happened exactly the way I tell it, but it is a true story nonetheless."

This collection has been culled from a preaching career that spans four decades. These sermons are not the polished essays of a scholar or the profound reflections of a sage. They simply trace the meandering of a pastor through forty years of parish ministry within the ever changing contexts of those years. They reflect my penchant for indirection and my fondness for the tacit dimension of experience.

If there is anything of use or value in this book, credit must go to the congregations I have been privileged to serve. Their wisdom (and forbearance) have contributed much to my spiritual growth and professional development. It must also go the staffs of these same congregations. Their competence, dedication and fellowship have inspired me, and their support helped make these years of ministry enjoyable and deeply satisfying. I am grateful to my colleagues in ministry and my partners in interfaith and community endeavors. They have kept me focused on the relevance of the preached word to a changing world. I always will be grateful to my friends and family who walk with me on this journey, know me intimately, and love me anyway.

I want to thank Weg Thomas for his thoughtfulness and great assistance with the production of this book, and Dave Inglis for his painstaking reading of the manuscript. I want to thank Michael Dennis Browne and the Collegeville Institute for Ecumenical and Cultural Research for their persistent calling forth of the writer within me.

Finally, I am indebted to those who have shared their struggles and deep gladness with me. In moments of vulnerability and grace we caught glimpses of the far-reaching hope that Easter embodies.

Weeping may endure for a night, but joy comes in the morning.

—Psalm 30:5

Between loss and hope

"Only Noah was left, and those that were with him in the ark. And the waters swelled on the earth for one hundred and fifty days." Genesis 7: 23b-24

    "God said, 'This is the sign of the covenant that I make between me and you and every living creature that is with you, for all future generations: I have set my bow in the clouds, and it shall be a sign of the covenant between me and the earth. When I bring clouds over the earth and the bow is seen in the clouds, I will remember my covenant that is between me and you and every living creature of all flesh; and the waters shall never again become a flood to destroy all flesh. When the bow is in the clouds, I will see it and remember the everlasting covenant between God and every living creature of all flesh that is on the earth.' God said to Noah, 'This is the sign of the covenant that I have established between me and all flesh that is on the earth.'" Genesis 9: 12-17

"In those days Jesus came from Nazareth of Galilee and was baptized by John in the Jordan. And just as he was coming up out of the water, he saw the heavens torn apart and the Spirit descending like a dove on him. And a voice came from heaven, 'You are my Son, the Beloved; with you I am well pleased.' And the Spirit immediately drove him out into the wilderness. He was in the wilderness for forty days, tempted by Satan; and he was with the wild beasts; and the angels waited on him." Mark 1: 9-12

1

We hardly can imagine what Noah felt in that haunting stillness. After days and nights of terror surely he felt relief, but also grief and fear, as he stepped from the ark for the first time.

In every direction as far as he could see there was devastation. Life had been extinguished; all life forms had perished from the earth except those few animals he managed to herd into the ark. Everywhere there was mud, rock and water. Everything familiar was gone. He was a stranger in a strange land, a refugee who could never return, an exile in a world he had not chosen.

Even God was heavy-hearted. Surveying the desolate landscape, six times God is heard to say, "Never again."

Though Noah's family were chosen as instruments of God—chosen to preserve and repopulate a now "purged" planet—their hearts were heavy, their shoulders stooped and their heads bowed as they stepped once more upon dry land. They were bewildered.

I have seen that bewilderment in the eyes of parents whose child was suddenly taken from them. In the eyes of a woman raped and abused, afraid of what more she must face. In the eyes of a young father with a promising career who learned that a brain tumor would deny him the future he had every right to expect.

Our Lenten journey begins here, in this poignant step between loss and hope, between the "no longer" of a life gone forever, and the "not yet" of a life yet to be. Here a covenant is created…a covenant after the Deluge, after the ruin, after the Holocaust. Here is a covenant between

God and all living things. Here is God's promise to protect and not destroy, to nurture and not diminish. Here God creates a covenant that extends to all sentient beings, a covenant of two words, "Never again."

❀ ❀ ❀

As Jesus approached the Jordan to be baptized by John did he, like Noah, teeter between grief and hope, loss and promise? As he stepped into the river, did he watch the innocence of his youth disappear upon the water? As he looked at the armed soldiers lining the shore, did he know what lay ahead for him? When the waters closed over him, was he overcome by the fear and promise of this moment? Did he expect a dove to descend? Did he expect to hear a voice resounding from heaven? Did he know what this meant, to be chosen and blessed by God?

In baptism, the sacramental becomes moral and the moral becomes sacramental. We prepare for what our ancestors called "spiritual warfare." To be chosen by God may be as much feared as welcomed. God's blessing is accompanied by joy and struggle, serenity and sacrifice. Immediately after his baptism Mark says that Jesus was "driven" by the Spirit into the wilderness for what sounds a lot like a vision quest.

Like Job, he was abandoned into the hands of Satan. No friends were with him. No family stood by him. Alone with the Prince of Darkness and Ruler of This World, temptations of glory, wealth and power were set before him to distract him from his mission.

Yet in this strange little story Jesus is not alone; he is "with the wild beasts," Mark says. "With" says Mark. There are echoes of the old covenant here—waters that purge, heavens that open, doves that bring signs, and once more the solidarity of sentient beings. Echoes, yes. But this time there is a clearer recognition of the subtle, facile, insidious, attractive and intractable presence of evil. The flood could not destroy it. Evil is present in the world and it is present in us—in our hearts and minds, in the worst among us, but also in the best. Jesus wrestled with the demons in himself before he challenged them in others.

In baptism, three promises converge. Three covenants are celebrated. Three levels of regeneration are proclaimed. First there is the Promise to Noah and a covenant with all sentient beings. It speaks of ecological harmony and a peaceable kingdom; God's blessing infuses all creation.

Then there is the Promise to Abraham, Sarah and Hagar, and covenants with particular households and peoples. These create standards of conduct and place ethical obligations upon us. In these covenants God's justice infuses our world.

Finally, there is the New Covenant revealed in Jesus Christ and inscribed upon our hearts. This is not an exterior blessing but an interior grace. It enables our deepest intimacy with God, our Beloved. With this covenant God infuses our life together with unconditional love.

When Jesus was baptized, these three covenants came together. In our baptisms too, we enter into these three sacred covenants—with all sentient beings, with the community of the faithful, and with the Holy One.

Noah and his family stepped off the ark. The world they knew was gone, yet they carried it within themselves. The new world was not yet here, but they bore it already within their imaginations. They began to re-create a world.

Jesus stood poised between the security of his past and the uncertainty of where his vocation would lead. In that moment he received his blessing and his call.

We ourselves live within the paradox of a vanishing past and an uncertain future. We do not know where our vocations will lead us. Our greatest risk is to take no risk. Each day we begin again.

Within every situation there is a possibility for grace—sheer, exuberant, unexpected grace. Grace that abounds. Grace that creates what we cannot anticipate. Grace that transforms everything. If we do not turn away, our Lenten path will lead us from loss to hope, from doubt to faith and from paradox into mystery.

Which way to the cathedral?

*"Mary Magdalene went and announced to the disciples,
'I have seen the Lord'; and she told them that he had said
these things to her."* John 20: 18

In 1984 Tenghiz Abuladze, a renowned Soviet director, created a film that altered the nature of political discourse in his country forever. It was called *Repentance*. For years the film languished in the can. Those who helped make it were fired for anti-Soviet activity. It took the intervention of Gorbachev himself to stop the censorious persecution and protect the director. The film was released about the same time the Chernobyl nuclear reactor exploded and with political consequences equally devastating.

It's the story of a corpse that won't stay buried. A Stalinesque character, Varlam is mayor of the city when he dies. He is buried with great ceremony. The next day the grieving city awakens to find his stiffened corpse leaning against a tree. He is reburied with dispatch, but on the following morning his corpse appears in a park. "We have to arrest the corpse," the officers say to the family, as they load it into a police wagon and drive off. He is reburied again. A protective metal cage is built over the grave; the door of it is padlocked. Police, with guns and attack dogs, take positions. That night a woman is captured as she begins digging at the grave.

"I confirm the facts, but I deny my guilt," she says at her trial. "For as long as I am alive, he will not lie in a grave. This sentence has been passed and is not subject to appeal. I will exhume him 300 more times if necessary."

What is this preoccupation? "It is not my wish to settle accounts with a dead man, but I have no choice in the matter." She tells the story of his rise to prominence and his exercise of power. It is a tale of intimidation, brutality, arbitrary arrests, exile, torture, executions, the separation of families, terror and endless persecution.

The guiding metaphor is the local cathedral. Once a place of divine worship and community celebration, the center for identity and purpose in the city, Varlam converted it into a production facility for nuclear weapons. This cracked the walls and foundations of the ancient building. Townspeople protested. The stones of the church contained their history, their values, their traditions, and their hope.

In response to their concern, Varlam spoke kind words and ordered a new facility built. Then he demolished the cathedral and had the protesters arrested. For telling this story, the woman is called criminal and insane. Crowds shout her down, but she remains firm. "On my own behalf, and on behalf of all innocent victims, I demand that Varlam Aravidze be exhumed by his kin.

"Aren't we to bury the dead?" they yell.

"No," she answers. "To bury him means to exonerate him. I say to you again: if you don't exhume him, I will. I won't leave him in the earth.

"How many times will you exhume him?" they ask.

"Until you stop defending him. Aravidze is not dead. For as long as you continue to defend him, he lives, and he continues to corrupt society.

Varlam's corpse keeps showing up at inopportune times and places: when a couple is making love, when a man is doing calisthenics. The re-appearance of the corpse is inconvenient, to say the least, and distressing for the townspeople. But it is embarrassing most of all. It is embarrassing because it becomes the material manifestation of Varlam's much more destructive presence in the minds and psyches of the people. Because they refuse to face the brutal facts of the past, he has all the more power over them. They are simultaneously victims and collaborators, survivors and sycophants, hardened and vulnerable. This "corpse that won't stay buried" represents all the unresolved, unrepented, shadowy, repressed pain and evil that locks people into a continuous bondage. It prevents their growth and true liberation.

In a way, the people had become corpses too—they are the dead trying to bury their dead, the unfeeling trying to bury their conflicted feelings, the un-alive trying to bury the cause of their alienation. Spiritually empty, they had lost faith in the future, lost confidence in the unknown, lost hope for a better world. All that was left was "to play the game", to "dance the dance of respectability" (Sartre)[1], "to put on the face to meet the faces that they meet" and "measure out their lives with coffee spoons" (T. S. Eliot)[2]. Unwittingly, they were choosing

---

[1] Jean-Paul Sartre, *Anti-Semite and Jew,* 1965, p. 84.

[2] T. S. Eliot, "The Love Song of J. Alfred Prufrock," *Prufrock and Other Observations,* 1917.

death over life, stagnation over novelty, cloying despair over spiritual rebirth.

The grave digger whom they called insane was the community's one voice of conscience. She was their witness. Her anguished appraisal actually promised new possibilities. She was saying that the way to gain freedom from past harm is to face it with courage. The way to be rid of the burdens we carry is not to admire them, not to defend them, not to bury them, but to acknowledge them and let them go.

Abuladze's film is powerfully specific to contemporary political realities in the U.S.S.R. Yet he has exposed a theme more breathtaking and universal than perhaps even he dreamed of. There are many "Varlams" buried in our consciousness—sins unadmitted, pain unacknowledged, evils unexplored. Their existence corrupts us. They isolate us. They divide us. They threaten to overwhelm us. They enervate and paralyze us. They draw their power from our fear of them. There is but one way to be free of their control: *Repentance.*

Contrast Abuladze's story with another: Another time. Another world of violence and corruption. Another age of deceit and spiritual hunger. Another death. Another burial. Another tomb. Another armed guard stationed to keep the corpse in its grave. Another woman as witness.

Are there not striking similarities with our Easter story? Yet there are differences too. Jesus is called "King" in three languages, but he is publicly scorned and only secretly mourned. He is cursed, rebuked, abused and abandoned by friend and foe alike. He is laid in a borrowed grave by a few remaining friends. Those who attend to his last needs have abandoned any pretense of playing the game. They are dropouts from the respectable dance. They have put aside their masks.

On the third day this grave also is empty. But she is no grave digger, this woman who approaches his tomb. There is no bitter resentment in her tears, no untold story and no corpse to be exhumed. There is no stiffened body leaning against a tree. Only sweet oils, clean linens and fragrant perfumes. This is a love story—the pathos of love lost, the exultation of love triumphant, the poignancy of love regained.

In the Easter story Life reaches into the maelstrom of intrigue, violence and death. With gentleness, with an almost parental love, Life reclaims its child from the Pit. It tenderly grasps him, warms his broken body and heals his wounded spirit. It rescues him from darkness and the eternal loneliness of the grave.

The stone is rolled away; all evidence of the power and terror of death are gone. The morning sun warms the garden, fragrant with dew-dripping flowers. A messenger of life awaits those who come to cleanse the body. "Why do you look for the living among the dead? He is not here. He goes before you even now into Jerusalem.

The woman runs to tell others. She has seen the worst that death can do; now death itself has been conquered. "Where, O death, is your victory? Where, O death, is your sting?"[3] The grave violates and demeans all that we

---

[3] I Corinthians: 15:55

cherish, but the grave itself has been vanquished. Its power has been diminished. This is no requiem—no "may he rest in peace." There is no sad bowing to the inevitable, no Stoic endurance of bitter gall. Death's stranglehold over creation has been broken.

Through Jesus, Life proclaims hope to a world still broken and conflicted. In him, henceforth, people will discover their true identities as children of Life. By him, people will be empowered to drop their masks and create their own dances. Walking with him, they will learn again that power and vitality are the gifts of Life to give. Following him, they will receive energy and purpose beyond their wildest comprehension.

At the conclusion of Abuladze's film, a bedraggled woman asks a resident, "Is this the road to the cathedral? Does this road lead to the church?"

"No," she is told. "This is Varlam Street. It does not lead to the cathedral.

"Well then, what's the use of it?" she says. "What good is a road that doesn't lead to the church?"

Many of us today are walking on Varlam Street. But we are searching for the road to the cathedral of authenticity. We are weary of dancing in a dance not of our choosing. We are "heavy laden" by the masks we wear.

Repentance, metanoia, conversion, paradigm shift, change of mind and heart, letting go—whatever we call it—this is the precondition for resurrection. This is the street we must find and walk. Repentance is the way to the cathedral. At the cathedral we will find our Easter joy

On "Repentance Street" we allow all that is dead within us to truly die. We let it go. We say good-bye. We repent of the harm we have done. We grieve what was, and what never will be. We acknowledge the emptiness and pain of our lot. We experience our fear, but we let go anyway. We let go of our powerlessness and shame. We let go of our despair and cynicism. We let go of our pain. We let go of our innocence and our guilt. We let go, trusting in the goodness of Life.

Trusting that in our free-fall, cut loose from all that is familiar, we will not be abandoned. Trusting that Life will reach into the maelstrom of our own time, place and circumstance, catch us in flight, hold us gently, and tenderly restore us to life. Trusting that we again will enjoy life among the living. Trusting that again we shall walk among the seeing. Trusting that we shall live among those who cherish the gifts of life. Trusting that at last we shall enter the cathedral.

What is the difference between a corpse that won't stay buried, and resurrection?

Repentance.

Easter happens on the other side of repentance.

The sorcerer within the walls

"A very large crowd spread their cloaks on the road, and others cut branches from the trees and spread them on the road. The crowds that went ahead of him and that followed were shouting, 'Hosanna to the Son of David! Blessed is the one who comes in the name of the Lord! Hosanna in the highest heaven!' When he entered Jerusalem, the whole city was in turmoil, asking, 'Who is this?' The crowds were saying, 'This is the prophet Jesus from Nazareth in Galilee.'"
Matthew 21: 8-11

The scene is familiar.

NOISE: People pressed against each other in the crowded streets of the walled city of Jerusalem. Vendors touted their wares. Soldiers barked their orders. Street-corner evangelists proclaimed their particular versions of impending doom. Children ran in every direction. All the world had gathered here to celebrate Pesach; every tongue could be heard in the cacophony of that day. Black Ethiopians bargained with white Irish soldiers; brown-skinned Nubians jostled olive-complexioned Palestinians for a place at the Temple gate.

ANIMALS: Sweating mules, horses and camels pushed their way through the human mass, while dogs, cats, goats, and chickens scurried underfoot. The presence of so many animals, laboring under heavy burdens, added a pungent aroma to the Middle Eastern morning air.

SMELLS: Open fires, roasting meat, human perspiration, olive oil used universally as a body ointment, aromatic pines, cedars and flowering plants, raw blood of slaughtered animals—all these greeted the first-time visitor as she made her way through the streets.

TENSION: Extra soldiers were stationed unobtrusively in the market. Priests and bankers furrowed their brows as they went about their work. Everything appeared normal, and yet…festivity mingled with fear; fear added a tinge of expectancy to all the festivities of this day.

ACTION: A parade! A spectacle! A demonstration! Coats, scarves and palm fronds waved emphatically in the distance. Undulating like the sea at high tide, the crowd began to move in waves toward this latest distraction. People stretched to see what was happening. The murmur turned into a contagious roar. The storm swept in all directions over the surface of the crowd. They could see a quiet figure at the center of all the excitement. Riding on a mule, dressed modestly in homespun clothes, he moved slowly through the gates and into the city.

The Sorcerer had arrived. His little band of apprentices surrounded him. The people squeezed around him. "The Sorcerer is here! The Sorcerer has come to Jerusalem! Do magic, Sorcerer! Show us your stuff, Sorcerer! Sorcerer, give us a show!"

It was not the first time that the tradition of the Sorcerer has been misunderstood. Nor would it be the last. Even today, the dictionary defines sorcery as "the use of power gained from the assistance or control of evil spirits". No one in primitive society was more remote than the Sorcerer. He or she lived beyond the walls of the ancient city. The Sorcerer practiced his or her arts within the greatest privacy. By choice or by calling, the Sorcerer abandoned the common-sense definitions of reality shared by his or her compatriots. At the same time, he or she staked out a refuge in a larger—spiritual—universe.

The Sorcerer inhabited two homes, two worlds, two realities simultaneously. To those who lived in the city, the Sorcerer's art was magic. They viewed it with wonder and alarm. But to the Sorcerer, it was a "technology" based on assumptions and hypotheses that seemed reasonable in the larger universe. To those within the city, the Sorcerer's practice was occult. But to the Sorcerer, the reality within the city was restricted and confining. Unlike the priest, the Sorcerer had no organization, no sanctions to apply. The authority of the Sorcerer lay precisely in the ambiguity that he or she embodied. The Sorcerer was an Alien, an Outsider and a Stranger.

We are attracted to—yet we fear—those who dwell beyond our walls: Our walls of conventional behavior, walls of nationality, walls of ethnicity, walls of class, clan, creed or culture—these walls are the boundaries of our self-definition. We like our walls. We need our walls. They organize the ambiguity of our existence. Psychologists tell us that these walls are necessary for our psychic survival. Within our walls we are secure.

Within the walls of our common experience we not only are secure, we are interdependent. Our resources are magnified by a synergistic effect. Within the walls of our shared assumptions, the dreadful loneliness which stalks us is kept at bay.

But walls that protect, imprison. Walls that structure our reality can stultify our growth. Walls that give us security, deny us mobility. Most of us are people who live within the walls. Xenophon, the Greek essayist and historian, once wrote that he could never understand why his contemporary, the philosopher Aristippus, "preferred everywhere to be an alien rather than imprison himself in a country."[4]

Yet great men and women have very often been aliens—or alienated—within their own society. They eat the same food, use the same language, and enjoy the same past-times. But, spiritually, intellectually or mentally they often seem to inhabit a different world.

Sometimes this is amusing to the rest of us. Jeremiah's tears brought laughter to his contemporaries. The authorities merely dismissed the eccentricities of John the Baptist—until he went too far. Beethoven's sonorities were derided by knowledgeable critics of his time. Albert Einstein's relativity theories initially were dismissed as the work of a second-class patent officer in Bern. Mother Theresa of Calcutta's ministry to the most destitute of the earth is viewed with condescension by revolutionaries and conservatives alike. While remaining physically present, each of these people left their spiritual homelands to occupy some part of a larger universe.

To a small degree, this may be a common experience. We know, for example, that the proverbial "absent-minded

---

[4] Xenophon, *Memorabilia*, 2.1.13. Another translation of "alien" here is "stranger-guest."

professor" is not mentally absent. She simply is mentally present elsewhere: in her own arcane world of computer programs, archeological digs, or Seventeenth Century Australian One-Act Plays. We all use the word "pre-occupied" to indicate that another and more pressing concern has asserted a claim on our attention.

Jesus was pre-occupied in the sense that a Sorcerer is pre-occupied. While he was in the world, he was not of it. While he was a Jew among Jews, he transcended not only Judaism but all organized religion. While he lived in history, history could not contain him.

James Joyce was a great novelist who breached the walls of literary and philosophical convention in his own time. He once said that his own existence was guided by three principles: exile, cunning and silence.[5] These are indeed the most salient qualities of the primitive Sorcerer.

When one thinks of sorcerers, one thinks of caves, forests, deserts, or mountains. Sorcery is practiced in the dead of night, unnoticed by the masses of humankind. The Sorcerer seems to inhabit a different reality. The Sorcerer's assumptions are not our assumptions. Indeed, we often fear and reject this Stranger in our midst. Jesus, the greatest Exile of all, once noted that a prophet is not accepted in his or her own country. The Sorcerer is an exile.

The Sorcerer is cunning. Did not Jesus admonish his disciples—shall we say "apprentices"?—to be wise as

---

[5] James Joyce, *Portrait of the Artist as a Young Man,* originally published in 1918.

serpents and gentle as doves? Did he not show an utterly this-worldly shrewdness that embarrasses his more pious interpreters to this day? Was he not cunning? "Cunning" is an old word for knowledge, of course. Because he is an outsider, the Sorcerer sees things we don't see, understands things we don't understand, and knows things we don't know.

Why do the Hebrew Scriptures require the respectful treatment of Strangers and Outsiders? Because they may be agents of God's revelation to the rest of us who are huddled within our family, ethnic and national walls. The Sorcerer introduces a note of objectivity into our subjective world.

Within the walls of convention, everyday language makes sense. Assumptions are shared, problems are identified, and meaning is communicated. But within this world, the Sorcerer often has no word to use, for the meanings he would convey do not fit into existing patterns of understanding. "One cannot put new wine into old wine-skins," Jesus was heard to say. Much of his teaching feels cryptic to us—hidden—not because he wished to hide it, but because the minds of his listeners were not yet big enough to grasp it. His parables, his koans, his answering questions with questions might be regarded as a kind non-response. The Sorcerer is silent.

Orlando Patterson has said that the ancient Sorcerer is the prototype of the individual, the one "who takes her own counsel", the one "who walks to the beat of a different drummer". The central truth and irony of the tradition of the Sorcerer is that she is human, "above all else human, and wholly human. The Sorcerer lives alone not because he despises humanity, but because he recognizes only humanity."[6] She will not be bound by the conventional distinctions that separate us. She inhabits not a different, but larger, reality. We may learn from the Sorcerer what it means to affirm the full measure of our humanity.

Howard Thurman was fond of the story of an Indian chief who was interviewed by a sociologist. "Are you a Canadian first, and then an Indian, or are you an Indian first, and then a Canadian?" The chief's response was this: "I come from the north country. I live with the snow, the ice, the sharp wind in winter. I live with the streams, the sun, the blossoms in summer. These flow into me, and I flow into them. They keep me, and I keep them. I am part of them and they are part of me. I am not sure what you mean."[7]

Jesus would have liked that answer. He was a child of his time, but he inhabited a realm beyond time. He understood the realities of political power, prestige, wealth and privilege, but he knew even better their limitations. He was an enigma to his family, his friends, his compatriots and his enemies. He came, as Albert

---

[6] Orlando Patterson, "The Tradition of the Sorcerer" in *Ethnic Chauvinism: The Reactionary Impulse,* 1977, pp. 19-32.

[7] Howard Thurman, in *A Stranger Freedom, The Best of Howard Thurman on Religious Experience and Public Life,* (Walter Fluker and Catherine Tumber, editors) 1998, pp. 245-246.

Schweitzer observed, "unknown, without a name." Yet he invited all to follow him.

❀❀❀

The crowd wanted to know his secret. They wanted to know, "Who is that man?" They tried to pin a label on him and so make him familiar: "He's a prophet!" "He's from Nazareth!" "He's from Galilee!" "He's the Son of David!" Later they would call him, "King of the Jews".

How ironic. The only title he ever gave to himself, as far as we know, is "The Son of Man"—in today's English, "The Child of Humanity". To himself, he was not the "Son of David", not a "child of Israel", not even a "Nazarene". Every group was his group. Every community was his community. Every crowd was his crowd. He was kith and kin to us all. Yet he clearly said that all who chose to follow him would have to leave their labels and their familiar worlds behind.

Conventional wisdom advises, "Look out for number one." The Sorcerer says, "Greater love has no one than this, that she lay down her life for a friend." Conventional wisdom cautions, "Don't get mad. Get even." The Sorcerer responds, "Love your enemy as yourself." Conventional wisdom advises, "Assert yourself." The Sorcerer replies, "The first shall be last, and the last shall be first." Conventional wisdom warns, "Don't fall into the same trap twice." The Sorcerer counters, "Forgive seventy times seven times." Conventional wisdom recommends that we "get all we can while we can." The Sorcerer answers,

"Where your treasures are, there will your heart be as well." This "wisdom" only makes sense to those who move beyond the walls.

Jesus taught with his words and stories, and he revealed in his own person, a radical universalism. In reacting against rigidities of law and tradition, he developed a gospel that was quintessentially revolutionary. In his universe there were not Jews and Romans, slaves and free, males and females, handicapped and able-bodied, oppressors and oppressed, but all brothers and sisters together. He recognized the sacredness of every personality. He saw the divine grace within us all. He moved with a radical freedom among all people.

The Sorcerer then, is not an exile. He cannot be an exile. We are the exiles. We are exiled behind the walls of our own defensiveness. We are exiled from our true natures. The Sorcerer is free and invites us to freedom, to become what we truly are meant to be.

And so, today, we welcome the Sorcerer within the walls of our own being. We converge upon him with naïveté, curiosity, hope and a longing for release. As the events of history show (his history and our own), we are not without ambivalence. Yet the Sorcerer is loose in our midst. He has shown us life beyond the walls, and we will never be the same again.

I conclude with the words of Albert Schweitzer:

"He commands. And to those who obey Him, whether they be wise or simple, He will reveal himself in the toils, the conflicts, the sufferings which they shall pass through in His fellowship and, as an ineffable mystery, they shall learn in their own experience who He is."[8]

[8] Albert Schweitzer, *The Quest for the Historical Jesus,* originally published in 1906.

In this sign: the power of the cross

With the Rev. Dr. Sally Purvis[9]

"For the message about the cross is foolishness to those who are perishing, but to us who are being saved it is the power of God. For it is written, 'I will destroy the wisdom of the wise, and the discernment of the discerning I will thwart.' Where is the one who is wise? Where is the scribe? Where is the debater of this age? Has not God made foolish the wisdom of the world? For since, in the wisdom of God, the world did not know God through wisdom, God decided, through the foolishness of our proclamation, to save those who believe. For Jews demand signs and Greeks desire wisdom[10], but we proclaim Christ crucified, a stumbling block to Jews and foolishness to Gentiles, but to those who are the called, both Jews and Greeks, Christ is the power of God and the wisdom of God. For God's foolishness is wiser than human wisdom, and God's weakness is stronger than human strength." I Corinthians 1: 18-25

Budd (Gilbert Friend-Jones): During Lent we have reflected about the cross as a symbol of our faith. We have

---

[9]   Sally Purvis is the author of *The Power of the Cross: Foundations for a Christian Feminist Ethic of Community,* and *The Stained-Glass Ceiling: Churches and Their Women Pastors.* She currently is a Minister-in-Covenant with Central Congregational UCC, Atlanta, GA.

[10] Re "Jews and Greeks," Paul engages in a bit of unfortunate hyperbole here. He himself had a foot in both cultures and was writing to both "Jews" and "Greeks." At this time the church was beginning to differentiate itself from its Hebraic roots on the one hand and the surrounding Hellenistic culture on the other. We wish he had been more nuanced in his pronouncement.

considered how it has been understood by Biblical authors and Church theologians, in history and in Christian life. This has also been a lifelong interest of yours, Sally. You have written about the power of the cross. Today you will help us understand how an instrument of such abuse can become an instrument of redemption.

This is Palm Sunday. Today we remember Jesus entering Jerusalem on a donkey, as though claiming his sovereignty. He is hailed as king. Later he will be mocked with the same title. An outsider must wonder if this parade has more to do with pathos than power—with the real, raw power to get things done.

One of the most meaningful Sundays in the church year for me comes just prior to Advent: 'Christ the King Sunday'. It is the pinnacle toward which the rest of the liturgical year progresses. All that goes before prepares us to recognize Jesus Christ as sovereign of the world and of our hearts. It also is the portal through which we enter the new Christian year. It foreshadows the year about to unfold. It affirms in the most assertive manner possible that Jesus Christ is King, Lord, and Sovereign. It is a serious statement about serious power.

Palm Sunday tries to make this same declaration. But today there is ambivalence: a joyful side and an ominous undertone. Children sing, but a gallows stands in the wings. Today poses a question, not an affirmation. It questions the sovereignty of Jesus. Not "Christ the King!" but "Christ the King?" What kind of sovereign is this, riding on a donkey to the cheers of the oppressed and downtrodden? Why do the "powers that be" find him so threatening? Why are they so determined to destroy him? Where is his power? What kind of king or queen would consent to flogging, humiliation and execution in such a fashion? Where were his defenders? Where the legions of angels promised to protect him?

Sally: Palm Sunday is deeply ambivalent; and it's more—it's ironic. Yes, there is a joyful side and an ominous undertone. Yes, children are singing and a gallows stands in the wings. And more—the crowds who shout hosanna today—because they think they've found their king, the powerful one who will lift the whole boat with them in it—these joy filled hosanna shouting Palm Sunday celebrants in just a few days will be shouting, "Crucify him, crucify him. Release Barabbas and crucify Jesus". Why? Because they were disillusioned. They felt betrayed. They were frightened and confused. This wasn't the power they were looking for. Then it all got overturned again three days later. It's enough to make us dizzy, trying to understand what happened.

Christ the King? That's one of my least favorite Sundays in the church year, unless, of course, it drips with the irony of Palm Sunday. Christ the King? That is the question, and the only way we can answer in the affirmative is to understand "kingship" in a whole new way, a way that turns ordinary understanding upside down. A way that can make sense out of sayings like, "The first shall be last and the last first." Or, "What does it profit us to gain the whole world and lose our soul?" Or, "God's ways are not our ways." We have to understand power in a whole new way to make any sense at all of Jesus' message and God's power.

Worldly power is so encumbering, so consuming, and so fragile. It takes so much to acquire power and so much to retain it. The slightest mistake, the smallest slippage, and it's over. Just ask Martha Stewart.

There's another example from contemporary history of one of the world's most powerful men who lost power, was disgraced in his loss of power, and who emerged into new prominence with a new kind of power, not of ruling but of giving. The man is Jimmy Carter.

Jesus was so free. He was connected and committed, but he was so free. The power he had was a gift, and it was worth everything to him, even his own life, even his own mission and visions and projects. How can that possibly make sense?

The most succinct statement of the reversal of our notions of power is Paul's first letter to the Corinthians: "For the message about the cross is foolishness to those who are perishing but to us who are being saved it is the power of God." And a bit further on, "For Jews demand signs and Greeks desire wisdom, but we proclaim Christ crucified... For God's foolishness is wiser than human wisdom, and God's weakness is stronger than human strength." I commend to your reading the rest of I Corinthians 1.

Here, I think, is the heart of the irony of Palm Sunday, and of the power of the cross: wherever we begin, we end up being directed away from ourselves, our need to influence and impose our wills, our need for power, and we are direct-

ed toward God, toward life, toward the reality of God's love. The power of the cross is the most counter-cultural reality there is. Jews demand signs, Greeks demand wisdom, Americans demand military superiority and a continually expanding economy. And then there's God's power.

It's far easier to say what the power of the cross isn't than to say what it is, but let me try. It's the power of life, of healing, of reconciliation. And the claim, anyway, is that that power, that force, is stronger than all the kings and armies and cultures there ever were or will be. Do we really believe that? Sunday after Sunday we say we do. Do we really?

Budd: Kurt Vonnegut wrote about power and violence in Slaughter House Five. An extraterrestrial student of Christianity supposed that the intent of the Gospels was to teach people to be merciful, even to the lowest of low. "But," he said, "the Gospels actually taught this: *Before you kill somebody, make absolutely sure he isn't well connected...* . The flaw in the Christ stories, said the visitor from outer space, was that Christ, who didn't look like much, was actually the Son of the Most Powerful Being in the Universe. Readers understood that, so when they came to the crucifixion, they naturally thought, 'Oh, boy—they sure picked the wrong guy to lynch that time!'"

Is that what happened? Is Jesus the lamb among wolves, or superman in disguise? The ram advancing inexorably toward slaughter, or the most well-connected human being in history?

In our world, sovereignty and power are associated. Queens, Kings, Sovereigns and Lords retain privileges only as long as they retain power. History is full of royalty discarded when the reigns of power slip from their grasp. Power means being able to impose one's will and to achieve one's purposes.

Power comes in many forms from many sources. It can be as benign as influence, or as violent as lethal force. It can be economic, political, intellectual or even personal. Power compels. Generally it is good to have power, and bad to lack it. We are not called to be powerless, but to be stewards of the power and influence that is ours. With enough power we can accomplish great things. With no power we can accomplish nothing. But if we reject Constantine's use of the cross as a symbol of conquest[11], then it is hard to see how Jesus' cross symbolizes anyone's power but Rome's. Once nailed to the cross, Jesus was powerless even to move his limbs or care for his basic needs. The cross was an instrument of torture that robbed him of his life. What kind of power is this?

Sally: Jesus was well connected all right. He had a "friend" so powerful that he could have turned stones to

---

[11] In 312 CE Constantine moved against Maxentius at the Plain of Milvian outside the gates of Rome. The story has survived that Constantine sought aid from the gods and was rewarded by the appearance of a flaming cross. In a dream he heard these words: "by this sign, conquer." The next day his troops went into battle bearing crosses on their shields or carried before them. They were victorious and Constantine emerged as the sole and first "Christian" ruler of the Roman World.

bread and fed every hungry person in the world.[12] Imagine how many lives would have been saved and good deeds done. He was so well connected, he could have been a king, a king like Herod, King Jesus, over all the known world, with a crown of gold on his head instead of a crown of thorns. He would then have been able to rule with perfect justice. Or, his powerful connection could have arranged for him to prove to the known world, through signs and miracles, that he was in fact the chosen one of God, and so many more people would have believed him. Why, he might not even have been crucified. Wouldn't his acceptance of even one of Satan's offers have been a better use of his potential than dying on a cross, alone, betrayed, humiliated? Wouldn't he have been a better steward of the gifts and powers God gave him?

Why didn't he accept his powerful friend's offers, or at least one of them? What in the world would he have had to give up that would have been more valuable than these stunning vocations? Those questions lead us right into the power of the cross; what we find there, every time, is God. Jesus' rejection of Satan's powers left him filled with the power of the Holy Spirit. The gospels don't deny that Satan is powerful, or that rulers are, or soldiers. They just tell us, in large ways and small, that God's power is different.

Jesus renounced all of Satan's wonderful offers and preached to his disciples about being servants. You think

---

[12] See Matthew 4:3: *"The Tempter came and said to him, 'If you are the Son of God, command these stones to become loaves of bread.'"*

you want to lord it over everyone? I tell you that you need to aspire to be servants to everyone. Budd, you asked, "What kind of power is this?" It's not our power. It's not something we can own or control or collect or preserve. It's just something we can join, seek to be part of, and try to reach for, again and again and again.

Budd: In many circles, this "Servant-King" is a big disappointment. Fyodor Dostoevsky eloquently described the intense frustration Jesus brings to the powerful in his chapter on "The Grand Inquisitor" in *The Brothers Karamazov.* Jesus came back to earth, only to be captured and brought before ecclesiastical authorities for interrogation. He wanted to bring spiritual freedom, they acknowledged, but the masses craved security and the basics of life. They argued, persuasively, that his way is ineffective and worse, and that it has taken centuries to undo the damage he had done. One cannot accomplish anything of significance, proclaimed the Inquisitors, from a position of powerlessness. The real Jesus had to be silenced forever!

Sally: I spoke before of the power of the cross as life, healing, reconciliation. There is an image of this power, a stark, naked image, with which we are soon to be confronted again: a corpse sealed in a rock. Is there any image more lifeless than a corpse sealed in a rock? Even death is often not as dramatically lifeless as this. The corpse wasn't buried in the ground where it would eventually decompose and become part of the natural process of life. It wasn't dropped into the sea where it would nourish life there. When we were in India we visited Varanasi and saw the funeral pyres along the shores of the Ganges and watched as the ashes floated, blown by the wind, into the holy river, rich in minerals and the potential of fertility.

With Jesus, the most powerful empire in the world had exerted its force. The religious authorities had exerted their significant influence. All promise was snuffed out; this man's beautiful words and were deeds gone. Dead and buried. A corpse sealed in a rock. And from this starkest of all images we get our clearest picture of the power of the cross. From utter lifelessness—life emerged, or so we claim.

Paul said in I Corinthians, "If Christ has not been raised, your faith is futile and you are still in your sins." The greatest powers in the world could seal a corpse in a rock, but they were helpless to bring forth life.

Is the power of the cross real? Is there a power abroad that is not in our grasp, not coercive, not human, not institutional, not owned even by the church, but that permeates all life, suffuses our lives, brings forth life and love and healing even after human power has done its worst? Is there something so valuable that the most benevolent and influential work a human could do, feeding the hungry, ruling the world in perfect justice, proving to everyone that you are the messiah, is worth renouncing?

As you watch this man ride into Jerusalem on a donkey, take these questions with you. As you move through the end of Lent into Holy Week, take these questions with you. Is there a power greater than that the world can teach you? Is the power of the cross the power of life? Does the cross lead us into the arms of God, over and over again? Did life emerge from that corpse sealed in a rock?

May God's power be with you on your journey through Holy Week.

Will the dust praise you?

"To you, O Lord, I cried, and to the Lord I made my sup-plication: What profit is there in my death, if I go down into the Pit? Will the dust praise You? Will it tell of your faithful-ness? ...O Lord, be my helper: You have turned my mourn-ing into dancing; You have loosed my sackcloth and girded me with gladness that my soul may praise You and not be silent. O Lord, I give thanks to You forever." Psalm 30: 8-12

W. H. Auden once said that death is like the distant roll of thunder at a picnic.[13] We hear its constant presence rumbling in the background. We feel helpless before it. We fear its arrival. We try our best to ignore it and hope it will pass us by. But we know it will rain; the outing will be disrupted. We know that death is inevitable and for each of us the picnic will only last so long.

In our more thoughtful moments, we ponder why this is so. With the Psalmist we ask, "What profit is there in my death, if I go down into the Pit? Will the dust praise You? Will it tell of Your faithfulness?" What good will be served? What is the meaning of death? If there is not a "meaning" to death, can there be a meaning to life?

These are among the most important questions we shall ever ask. They have been raised by sincere and thoughtful people in every generation. Yet the answer, if there is one, evades us, and the evidence is ambiguous.

Some of us have long since reconciled ourselves to the inevitability of dying. We have decided to do the best

---

[13] W. H. Auden, *Marginalia*, composed between 1965 and 1968.

we can in the limited time we have. We live as though our lives were merely matches struck against a great and cosmic darkness. We act as though our consciousness, our affections, our thoughts, our beliefs and our aspirations— all these—are but aberrations of nature. Here today, gone tomorrow—of no enduring value and soon to be extinguished forever.

"You only live once," I have heard more than once. "Eat, drink and be merry," we say, "for tomorrow we will die." What's missing is appreciation for the idea that our life on earth may be for the purpose of soul-building, of equipping ourselves for eternity. We sum up our whole philosophy of life in the first few words of the Christian burial liturgy: "Earth to earth, dust to dust, ashes to ashes." We say much less about the concluding words of the service: "the hope of the resurrection and life everlasting."

The great British philosopher Bertrand Russell raised this rather limited understanding to the level of a metaphysical principle:

"...all the labour of the ages, all the devotion, all the inspiration, all the noonday brightness of human genius are destined to extinction in the vast death of our solar system...the whole temple of (our) achievement must inevitably be buried beneath the debris of a universe in ruins...only on the firm foundation of unyielding despair can the soul's habitation henceforth be safely built."[14]

---

[14] Bertrand Russell, "A Free Man's Worship", *Mysticism and Logic*, 1917, pp. 45-46.

"Earth to earth, dust to dust, ashes to ashes." That is what Dr. Russell is saying. That is what many of us believe. We look out on a universe whose immense night defies our comprehension. We look back over a bloody history that defies humane explanation. We look within our own private and busy lives; we mistake the surfaces for the depths. We plan our little picnics and hope it won't rain.

We may accept such a fate with Bertrand Russell's dignity and humor. We may seek to escape its awful verdict by living through our children or our institutions. We may amass great estates or make lasting contributions in our chosen fields. Yet we recognize truth in Russell's somber sentences. We too know how the caged bird feels, and why it beats its wings and sings.[15]

We refuse to become accustomed to our cage and never think of freedom. We refuse to be prisoners who regard our cells as our only home. We refuse to be cave dwellers who never see flowers and sunlight.

We refuse to go meekly into that good night. We want to know if there is more. We are wayfaring strangers traveling through this world below, but we refuse to abandon our quest. We are prodigal daughters and sons who have come to a far country, but we crave to know our true identities.

[15] Paul Laurence Dunbar, "Sympathy", *Lyrics of the Hearthside*, 1899. This poem and a subsequent poem by Maya Angelou that it inspired are strong protests against racial oppression. These poems also and aptly speak to the human condition.

Easter is not disconnected from our everyday experiences. Though rooted in antiquity, it celebrates the hope that springs anew with each flower and budding branch. Winter may have its day, when trees stretch skeletal fingers against freezing skies, but we know that beneath the snow, in the depths of the earth, life stirs and prepares to burst forth.

Everyday, at every point in our lives, we are surrounded and sustained by mystery. Why is there something and not nothing? We take too much for granted. We rarely marvel that we marvel. We rarely question that we question. We assume so much.

Yet we believe that God made nothing in vain and loves all that she has made. On Easter we dare to affirm that even the dust shall praise God. Easter is the harbinger, the precursor, the messenger. Easter is the promise that, despite Ecclesiastes and Bertrand Russell, all is not vanity.

Loren Eiseley was one of this century's great naturalists and poetic spirits. While on an archeological expedition in the American Badlands, he got lost. It was a cold windy day as he climbed a barren hill to get his bearings. The sun was going down. From the north he saw a great swarm of birds coming toward him. Their faint wild twittering filled the desert air. He later wrote,

"I lifted up a fistful of that ground and held it while that wild flight of south-bound warblers hurtled over me into the oncoming dark. There went phosphorous, there went iron, there went carbon, there beat calcium in those hurrying wings. Alone on a dead planet I watched that incredible miracle speeding past. It ran by some true compass over field and wasteland. It cried its individual ecstasies into the air until the gullies rang. It swerved like a single body...

"I dropped my fistful of earth. I heard it roll inanimate back into the gully at the base of the hill: iron, carbon, the chemicals of life... As I walked into my camp late at night, one man... asked sleepily, 'What did you see?'

"'I think a miracle,' I said softly, but I said it to myself."

Even in his scientific work, Eiseley experienced a Presence moving through creation, a sacred vitality that assumed a thousand countenances, a spirit seeking self-expression through the evolutionary process. "We forget," he once observed, "that nature itself is one vast miracle transcending the reality of night and nothingness." In a way he was saying that dust—"the chemicals of life"—does praise.[16]

John Wheelock was an American poet with a similar reverence and sense of wonder. He too believed that what is, is not obvious. Matter clothes spirit as spirit directs matter.

[16] Loren Eiseley, *The Immense Journey*, 1957, pp. 170-173.

"Here in my curving arms I cup
This quiet dust; I lift it up.
Here is the mother of all thought;
Of this the shining heavens are wrought,
The laughing lips, the feet that rove,
The face, the body that you love;
Mere dust, no more, yet nothing less.
All this has suffered consciousness,
Passion, and terror, this again
Shall suffer passion, death and pain.
For as all flesh must die, so all,
Now dust, shall live. 'Tis natural;
Yet hardly do I understand—
Here in the hollow of my hand
A bit of God I keep
Between two vigils fallen asleep."[17]

"Will the dust praise You? Will it tell of your faithfulness?"
All creation groans in travail wrote St. Paul. All creation
is in bondage to decay. All creation longs for liberation.[18]
Our Easter affirmation is not only that our separate, ego-
centric selves will be saved from the clutches of the grave,
but that all creation will be redeemed. The silence of death
will be broken and all creation will give thanks:

---

[17] John Hall Wheelock, "This Quiet Dust" in *Modern American Poetry*, 1962, p. 334.

[18] Romans 8: 18-23.

"Let the heavens be glad, and let the earth rejoice;
let the sea roar, and all that fills it;
let the field exult, and everything in it.
Then shall all the trees of the forest sing for joy."[19]

Many of you know that my wife is an artist. Her studio is located in our house. I am immensely curious about her work, so I often go there to see what she is producing. When she creates a work of art, she follows a process that involves many stages over an extended period of time. One stage suggests the next to her, but it doesn't make much sense to me. To produce a single work of art requires a great deal of patience.

I am, by nature, less patient than she. So I constantly ask her questions. "When will it be finished?" "Why are you doing that?" "What are you going to do next?" "What will it be like when you are done?"

My wife is very patient, as I've said, and not only with her art work. Sometimes she suggests that I go somewhere else and work on my sermon. At other times she just smiles. She really can't answer all my questions, because her work evolves in a kind of dialogue between herself and her materials. She works with an easy and steady confidence, secure in the knowledge that beneath her brush something of significance will result.

---

[19] Psalm 96.

Only when she has finished, only when the work has been matted and framed, only when we can stand back and see the completed piece, only then, do all the previous stages make sense. At the end of the process I can look back and say, "Now I see why she did that." Those seemingly disconnected applications of paints, inks and color fields assume a new significance when the work is done.

I wonder if all creation, all history and all the individual stories of our lives are really "works in progress" or —more likely—parts of a single great work of creation? And we, like impatient husbands, are always wanting to know, "When will it be finished?" and "What will it be like when it is done?"

The picture is not finished. Shall we despair?

Shall we despair if "now we see in a mirror dimly" and "now we know only in part"?[20]

Shall we despair when it rains on our picnic?

No, for we know that the sun will follow the rain as surely as day follows night. As surely as the warm winds of spring follow the icy deadness of winter. We live an Easter vision that speaks of earth, dust and ashes, but also of hope, resurrection and life everlasting. We believe that one day all creation—even the dust—will praise God.

---

[20] I Corinthians 13: 12.

When Easter interrupts

"What is sown is perishable, what is raised is imperishable. It is sown in dishonor, it is raised in glory. It is sown in weakness, it is raised in power." I Corinthians 15: 42b-43

"Maundy Thursday I can understand. Good Friday is tragic, but real. But Easter? Easter seems contrived and forced. It doesn't connect with my experience." These are not uncommon words around our church. For some of us, Easter can be a difficult holiday.

Today's celebration confronts many modern people with a huge dilemma. Our Christian ancestors regarded Easter as the cornerstone of our faith. Take it away, and the whole structure collapses. As the apostle Paul said in the first letter to the Corinthians, "If Christ be not risen, then preaching is useless and believing is in vain." Paul recognized that this message was "folly" to those who would be wise. The early Church was unanimous in affirming that God acted at Easter in a unique and miraculous way, defying 'natural law,' upending the created order, and challenging basic assumptions about life and death. This belief, whether simplistic and literal, or nuanced and metaphorical, has animated Christians from that time to this.

The faith of Easter has given *hope* to generations of enslaved and oppressed peoples from Soweto to Zinovievsk, from San Salvador to Saint Paul. It has enabled people to endure unspeakable hardships with courage, to overcome demeaning and destructive circumstances with dignity, to persist in their struggles against overwhelming

43

force, and finally to emerge victorious with their humanity intact, and their hearts and minds opened to a more compassionate social order.

The faith of Easter has given *comfort* to generations of grieving people. From Bethlehem, Judea, in 93 CE, to Bethlehem, Pennsylvania, in 1993 CE, sorrowing friends and family members have gathered—under sun and under rain, by day and by night—to mourn, to remember, and to hope. They have been consoled by their faith that nothing of true and intrinsic worth is ever lost, and that love shared is stronger even than separation imposed by death.

The faith of Easter has given *encouragement* to generations of questing people. From Nablus to Novosibirsk, from Jericho to Tokyo, thoughtful people have meditated on the brevity of human existence. They have concluded that our "four score and ten" years is more a launching than a limit. They have come to believe that our conscious life is but a small part of the soul's infinitely larger journey.

While some may conclude that the purpose of life is "to eat, drink and be merry," others are preparing themselves for wider seas. Even so, it is very difficult for thoughtful, sensitive and compassionate people today to affirm resurrection with integrity.

There are the obvious arguments against resurrection based on common sense. People are not raised from the dead. People don't re-appear. Corpses are not reanimated. The evidence is overwhelming that the dead stay dead. Indeed, it would be very unsettling to us if it were otherwise. Although sometimes we fear our own deaths, or deeply grieve the losses of loved ones, we accept that death is an inevitable part of life. We build the assumption of mortality into the very structure of our societies and the fabric of our communities. Death brings change, and change—it must be said—renews and reinvigorates life.

Many liberal Christians try to reconcile the importance of Easter and the dictates of common sense. We interpret Easter as recognition of the springtime renewal of life. I myself have published articles demonstrating the dependence of many Easter customs on cults of the ancient world. The prayer we used earlier in the service, from the Congregational worship book of 1948, goes far in this direction.

We may become patronizing. We treat the ancient writers as "primitive". We assert that they were writing theology and not history, myth and not fact. Never mind that they went to great lengths to name creditable witnesses and to refute the arguments of common sense, which were as persuasive then as they are now. Many today would remake Christianity into a kind of nature cult. Together with the greeting card industry, we would turn the greatest feast day of the Christian faith into a sentimental affirmation of the rhythm of the seasons.

This is not without value. We are children of the earth, and we participate in its rhythms. In an agrarian society, perhaps this transformation was inevitable. Many of our Easter customs did, in fact, derive from fertility religions that pre-date our Christian faith. We have only to look at the abundance of bunnies, flowers and eggs to recognize the perpetuation of ancient practices into present times. But how much hope does the "return of springtime" give to people who are sorely oppressed? How much comfort does "evidence of new life" give to those who are grieving extraordinary losses? How much encouragement does a "religion of nature" give to those who hunger and thirst for righteousness? Not the victory of Life over Death, but the oscillation between life and death, is what such a religion is willing to affirm.

There is another and deeper argument against Easter, however, and I would touch on it now. It is a persuasive argument. It is an argument our century may be uniquely qualified to make. It really is an argument against faith, against love, and against God. Oddly, it is an argument based on compassion and fellow feeling. It is based on sensitivity toward others and appreciation for the diversity of life on earth. The evidence to sustain this argument comes from our daily newspapers and news broadcasts. It comes from killing fields and concentration camps. It comes from rat-infested apartments and crack houses, and from alleys stained with the blood of innocent victims.

It challenges us through the unseeing eyes of starving children. It asserts itself in the unspoken fear of women in parking ramps, and of children when "Daddy has been drinking". The employee who is summoned to the boss's office when the company is down-sizing, the teenager who discovers she is pregnant, the activist who receives the fateful diagnosis—all these have encountered this argument first hand. With empires collapsing, deficits expanding, and terrorism rising, this argument reaches an astonishing crescendo. It gives words like bigotry and violence their power. If Christ be risen, how could this world continue to be? If Christ be risen, why does the suffering of innocents multiply? If Christ be risen, when shall death be overcome?

From a global perspective, the great and secular hopes for humankind announced at the beginning of our century[21] seem to be collapsing at its end. Martin Heidegger, one of our century's pre-eminent philosophers, proclaimed that the human being is a "being-unto-death." Flannery O'Connor has written that we have domesticated despair. St. Paul, perhaps you were wrong. The sting of death is very real. The grave appears to have the victory.

"If Christ be not risen, then preaching is useless and believing is in vain." If Christ be not risen, then our hope is misplaced, our comfort is false, and our encouragement is ill begotten. If Christ be not risen, then a courageous Stoicism, not an adventurous faith, is called for.

If Christ be not risen. That is a very big "if". An awesome "if". So much hangs upon it.

If it is of any consolation, our own confusion over Easter is reflected in the pages of the gospels themselves. Some texts are laced with realistic touches. Others are

---

[21] The Twentieth. Consider, for example, Edward Bellamy's classic, *Looking Backward*, with its message of inevitable progress.

contradictory. The earliest version of the earliest gospel (Mark) is striking for its brevity. Mark gives many believable details about the trial of Jesus, and about his execution. But Mark says almost nothing about a resurrection. Three women (who are identified) find the tomb opened. Inside a white-robed youth (not an angel, and not identified) tells them that Jesus has been raised and has gone before them. In Galilee they will see him, as he promised. Mark ends his gospel with these very believable words: "And the women came out and ran away from the tomb, frightened out of their wits, and they said nothing to a soul, because they were afraid."[22]

Other texts reveal the confusion of the authorities, the religious leaders, the people, the friends and family close to Jesus, and his followers. They also were unwilling or unable to accept the reality of a living Christ. Grief and tragedy they understood. A miscarriage of Roman justice they fully apprehended. But a resurrected Christ played havoc with their sense of the order, constancy and predictability of nature.

After Jesus died, the disciples prepared to return to their families and former occupations. They had enjoyed an exciting few years with him; their lives no doubt were changed. There would always be a special place for Jesus in their hearts. These had been their glory days, when they were young and foolish, when they played with fire

---

[22] *Jerusalem Bible*, Mark 16:8. Most scholars agree that Mark 16:9-20 are later additions to the original work.

and came close to getting burned. They would remember these days forever, even when their eyes grew dim, their hair white, and their knees began to crack.

When their grandchildren asked them about the "olden days" they would grow talkative and nostalgic. They would tell tall tales. Their euphoric recall of their time with Jesus would make them look brilliant. They would allow themselves wistfully to imagine what might have been. They would write memoirs. They might even achieve a little fame before they faded into history.

Perhaps the oral tradition would have kept their stories alive, and embellished them as they passed from generation to generation. Perhaps Jesus, "Rabbi Yeshua", would find a place in Jewish history along side other great rabbis like Hillel and Akiba whose wisdom has shaped the traditions. Perhaps not. Time would tell. That's how the story should have ended.

But Easter interrupted. However we choose to interpret the events of that week, whatever explanation we devise to satisfy our need for explanations, we cannot ignore one gigantic fact. A downward-spiraling, unraveling, disintegrating, depressing business-as-usual sequence was arrested. On that distant morning so long ago a new power escaped into the world. It began to challenge the death-assuming realities that prevail around us. It began to rewrite history. It began to transform lives. All of creation began to awake, as if from a long and troubled sleep.

Those who had lived timid lives of doubt began to live lives emboldened by a transforming affirmation. Those who were frightened became courageous. Those who had been tamed by their fear of death now dared openly to defy its power. A little rag-tag band of quarreling losers at a provincial outpost of a mighty empire began to engage the principalities and powers of their world. They opposed the hard steel of sword and spear with the tender inclusivity of a love that knows no bounds. They challenged the deification of state, race and market with a radical respect for all of the created order. They endured scorn and ridicule, the loss of home and work. Their families were endangered and they were persecuted. But when one fell, ten rose up, and the social and personal ethic of Jesus began to recreate the world.

There was nothing inevitable about Easter, nor is the final conquest of plowshare over sword a foregone conclusion. But on that Easter morning, a closed-in, stale, stifling, confining and familiar universe cracked open. On that Easter morning, the voice of the God of our ancestors once more resounded with clarity over all the planet: "I have set before you the choice of life or death, blessing or curse. Therefore choose life, that you and your descendants may live."

Each generation has found itself challenged by the militant, virulent power of Death, who still retains an awesome array of weaponry. Each generation has the choice thrust newly upon it: life or death, blessing or curse. Each generation, and every person, finds that Death has planted a cross between them and their ultimate fulfillment. Each of us returns to the tomb, scarcely able or willing to believe. Is it really empty?

The great Twentieth Century student of totalitarian systems, Hannah Arendt, wrote in her book, The Human Condition,

"The life span of humanity running toward death would inevitably carry everything to ruin and destruction if it were not for the faculty of interrupting it and beginning something new. (This is) a faculty which is inherent in action. (It is) an ever-present reminder that, though we must die, we are not born in order to die but in order to begin... Only the full experience of this capacity can bestow faith and hope on human affairs."[23]

"We are not born to die, but to begin." We are not "beings-unto-death." We are "beings-who-begin". Or more accurately, we are face-to-face with a choice of enormous consequence for ourselves and for the world. When confronted and harmed by the power of death, we are challenged to begin again. We begin again, knowing full well the cost, but also the promise, of our commitment.

The Living Christ breaks into our world with astonishing power. He declares that life is worth risking. He convinces us of life's loftiest purposes. When we are overcome by doubt or desperation, he calls us to hope. When we are overwhelmed by fear or depression, he

---

[23] Hannah Arendt, *The Human Condition*, 1958, p. 246.

refreshes us and restores our souls. When we are paralyzed by our despair, the reality of Easter empowers us to act.

Easter is God's greatest interruption.

"Well, there's always Easter!"

"On this mountain the Lord of hosts will make for all peoples a feast of rich food, a feast of well-matured wines, of rich food filled with marrow, of well-matured wines strained clear. And he will destroy on this mountain the shroud that is cast over all peoples, the sheet that is spread over all nations; he will swallow up death forever. Then the Lord God will wipe away the tears from all faces, and the disgrace of his people he will take away from all the earth, for the Lord has spoken. It will be said on that day, Lo, this is our God; we have waited for him, so that he might save us. This is the Lord for whom we have waited; let us be glad and rejoice in his salvation. For the hand of the Lord will rest on this mountain." Isaiah 25: 6-10

She was the epitome of controlled elegance as she waited to see the minister. She wore her hair in a stylish pixie cut with barely noticeable highlights. Her blue wool suit accented the blueness of her eyes. Her lip quivered ever so slightly as she tried to make conversation with the secretary. Soon he was off the phone and welcomed her into his office. A massive desk piled high with stacks of paper separated the two of them.

They had been friends for many years. He knew something was wrong when he got her urgent call. Within hours he had cleared his schedule to accommodate her. She barely had sat down when she started to weep profusely. Her mascara ran as she reached for the tissues he extended in her direction.

Within a freakish few hours she had received devastating news from three unrelated directions. At breakfast her husband told her he was leaving her for another woman. Around 9:30 a.m. her daughter called to tell her that her doctor had diagnosed a rare and irreversible congenital condition that would prevent her from ever having children. And at 11:00 a.m. her own gynecologist suggested that she had all the symptoms of cancer and should see an oncologist as soon as possible. She was alternately numb, panicked, outraged, confused, guilty, devastated, and alone. Her identity as a woman—and indeed as a human being—was under terrible assault.

Forty minutes and a box of tissues later, bits and pieces of her story now spread over the desk and covered the space between them. Still convulsed with heaving sobs of hopelessness, she looked at her friend. "Tell me something good," she said, "Anything! Tell me something hopeful!"

"Well," he said, not knowing what to say, "Well," he repeated, "There's always Easter."

A long silence ensued.

"Is that all?" she asked, not comprehending his helplessness before the story she had just unfolded. "Is that all?"

In truth, he didn't know what to say. The pain and desperation she was feeling had entered his own soul. His loss for words pointed more to the deep connection between them, to their long and cherished friendship, than toward his lack of pastoral skills. Without a doubt, had this interview been the final exam in Counseling 101, he would have fared poorly. Though she asked for words that were hopeful, she was not at a place where she could hear them. This was not the moment for a sermon, however brief. This was not, as they like to say, a "teaching moment." Indeed, at this moment there were no acceptable answers. None. Not even Easter.

Václav Havel once wrote from his prison cell "Hope is a state of mind, not of the world." He went on to say that hope, in a deep and powerful sense, is not the same as joy, not confidence that things are going well, not a willingness to believe that everything is heading for success. It is rather an ability to live for something because it is good. She had come to him seeking hope.

Believe it or not, in his stammering and inarticulate way I think her pastor had given her exactly this. He had communicated some very important messages to her: First, she was profoundly important to him. Second, her story had touched him so deeply that he knew not how to respond. Third, she was not alone and would not have to face this by herself. Fourth, as incomprehensible as it may have seemed to her at the time, this wrenching crisis was but part of a larger and deeper personal journey that could lead her into to a larger and deeper life. In essence, hope.

Without thinking at all, he had joined her in her depths, and from there reached into the core of their shared faith. He was grasping at its central affirmation: "Well, there's always Easter!"

These words sounded thin as they hung in the air between them. They were unconvincing to him even as he said them. They were unconvincing to her even as she strained to understand.

His timing was atrocious. She was standing on, shall we say, "this" side of Easter. At this moment in her life, "Easter" was inconceivable. Between her and the resurrection stood a huge and horrible cross. That was all she could see. It didn't even look like a cross. It looked like cancer. It looked like betrayal. It looked like her daughter's loss. She stared at her friend in disbelief.

But that really was all he could think to say.

Still she knew he cared. He was the first person she thought of when this morning crashed around her. She did not regret coming. She felt somewhat stronger having simply laid out in the space between them the geography of her crisis.

She asked for and received a prayer. She wiped away the tears and smudged mascara, replaced her lipstick, and rose to go. She knew it would be hard but she would get through it. One way or the other, she would manage. She knew also that she would be back. Though she suspected that she was a bit more reflective than he—or at least more "emotionally literate"—she would need him on this journey. She was absolutely confident that he would be there for her. She knew him well enough to know that he would call occasionally, tell her embarrassingly silly jokes to try to make her laugh, and drop her notes from time to time. She knew for certain that she could call him at any time and he would offer a sympathetic ear. But for now, she needed to see her daughter.

A few years later she told me this story. He had retired and moved away, but she carried the memory of that encounter deep within her. A single woman in her sixties, and the grandmother of a beautiful adopted daughter, she still was being monitored and treated for a persistent and pernicious cancer.

"You know," she said, "when he said 'There's always Easter' I thought that was the stupidest, most uncaring, unfeeling, distancing thing ever to come out of his mouth. I still think he didn't know what to say. It was stupid. But what do you say to a woman who has just dumped that load on you?

"But over the years I have come to understand that there is a cross in the very nature of things. Every person has to face some wrenching moment, some impossible situation, some awful decision between unacceptable alternatives. Between us and our desires there stands a cross…a stark, immutable, impossible, impassible cross. Life is not fair. Love makes us vulnerable. It all can be taken away in a flash. It all can be threatened in ways we can never imagine.

"At the very heart of everything we love," she said, "there is a cross. I don't know how else to explain it. There is vulnerability. There is suffering. There is sacrifice. There is a risk of hurt and harm and loss. I think I knew that going in.

"What I didn't know is this: At the very heart of suffering, there is love. Nothing opens one more to the exquisite, poignant, fleeting quality of this reality than the certain knowledge of one's mortality. When I am not nauseated from my treatments, I find myself savoring each day and each minute, the color blue and the rain against the window pain. I savor my time with my daughter and my time with you, and this cup of tea. I look at my cluttered living room and I see a still life composition; I savor that too. This is what I mean when I say that Jesus is my Savior; he savored life. He wants us to savor the life we have, and to distill the blessings packed into every moment.

"You know," she continued, "every religion has its symbols. Each symbol conveys something essential about how that religion sees life. The Star of David for example, has six points for the six ordinary days of the week. They all revolve around the center, which in Judaism is the Sabbath. The yin and yang of Taoism convey the coexistence and necessary balancing of opposites.

"Our symbol is the cross. Did you ever wonder why we chose that instead of, say, the fish? Or the manger? Or the shepherd's crook? The cross was a gruesome instrument of terror and death. Any fool knows that. But God transformed it into a symbol of reassurance and Life. That is not so obvious.

"The cross is not about suffering, but about love. Mel Gibson gets it wrong here. But love is not about a life without suffering. Jesus suffered so much because he loved so much. His suffering was much more than physical agony. He suffered in his soul. He suffered because he loved us. He loved this awful wonderful world we're condemned to inhabit. He suffered because we suffer, and because we don't see the beauty all around.

"Suffering in itself is never good. Personally, I would banish it forever from the world. But suffering can be a teacher, and it teaches what we seem unable to learn in any other way: To live the moments we have, and not grieve the moments we lack. To cherish the life we've got, and not curse the life that is missing. To take the unique qualities of our own little lives and make of them something lovely and something loving. Even in our suffering, to reach deep into our depths, to connect with the Spirit, to allow it to breathe and live through us. The cross is our most precious symbol for Life.

"'And there's always Easter!' Can you believe he actually said that! I thought he had lost it, the poor dear. My husband was leaving me, my daughter was grieving, and I was scared to death. And he said that! What did Easter have to do with anything?

"But you know what? He was right. Not the Easter most people know about. Not the Easter baskets, new clothes and colored eggs. Not even Jesus in the garden, if we think of that merely as the resuscitation of a corpse some 2000 years ago. But if we think of Easter as a kind of truth, as Truth, then yes, he was right. It is not a question of whether my life will go on forever or not. Of course it won't. I'll probably die of this cancer, or its cure. It won't be pretty, and I'll probably go kicking and screaming. It's not even a question of whether some vaguely disembodied spiritual form of me will go on forever. God forbid! I can't imagine even wanting that to be the case!

"I think Easter means that Life is alive! Life is not the same thing as my life, but my life inhabits this greater thing called Life. And it is alive. It is more alive than all the forces arrayed against it. It is alive and ceaseless. No punishment can destroy it, no suffering can squelch it, and no cross can overcome it. Life is there at the cross, on the cross. It was there in Jesus. It is there with each one of us as we face our struggles and deal with our pain. Life is alive, and it loves. It is dauntless in its loving. It is awesome in its power. It reveals to us a 'way out of no way' when we are most down. Life itself is the most amazing fact of life, of anybody's life.

"'There's always Easter!' I've come to believe this is completely true. This is utterly trustworthy. This is the fundamental premise upon which I have built my recovery. It is the basis of my life. I love that dear man for his awkwardness that day. He didn't know what to say, and so he said this. And these words stuck with me through all that followed. Through the awful divorce. Through my daughter's disappointment. Through my own therapy and treatments.

"It has become a cliché in my family. Now, whenever we get really bad news, we look at each other and say, 'Well, there's always Easter!' And you know what? There is. Always. Always Easter on the other side. Always a sun rising somewhere. Always a butterfly just waiting to break out of its cocoon. Always a new quality of life waiting for the hard protective shell to break. 'There's always Easter!' Always, for those who are able to see it.

"Did you know that Gerald Manley Hopkins used 'Easter' as a verb? 'Let him easter in us...' he wrote in a lovely reflection on a tragic accident.[24] That's exactly what happens. Just when we are most into our pain, our bewilderment, our hopelessness, just then a light begins to dawn. He Easters in us! And all our suffering, all our confusion and all our despair no longer are unbearable. They give way to something approaching hope. Not hope that a miracle will happen and everything will be made OK, but a hope that our lives—whatever their circumstances—will have meaning and connection. A hope that life, ultimately, is good."

I'd like to report to you that the last time I saw her was on an Easter Sunday. It would be fitting and dramatic, but it would not be true. I saw her last on my last Sunday in the church where she belonged. It was not an Easter Sunday as the calendar goes. Yet for her it was. Every Sunday has become an Easter celebration for her. Every day has become an Easter for her. But just as every day is a kind of Easter, yet each day continues to be Good Friday too. She manages to live in both realities simultaneously,

---

[24] Gerald Manley Hopkins: *Let him easter in us, be a dayspring to the dimness of us, be a crimson-cresseted east...* in "The Wreck of the Deutschland", Poems, 1918.

in both as fully as her strength allows, with deep joy and abiding peace. Jesus is her Savior, and I am sure she would want all of us today to savor the sheer goodness and wonder of life.

Happy Easter to you all!

My dancing day

A sermon for two voices and choir

"We piped for you, and you would not dance. We wept and wailed, and you would not mourn." Luke 7:32

Choir Sings:

Tomorrow shall be my dancing day,
I would my true love did so chance
To see the legend of my play,
To call my true love to my dance.

Sing O my love,
Sing O my love, my love, my love,
This I have done for my true love.[25]

Voice One:

The last two days had been hell for her. She had loved this man with all her being. For several years she had shared his life. She had walked the gritty roads of Galilee with him. The sun had beaten down on their cloaked heads. Rains had drenched their bodies. Breezes wafting off the sea had refreshed their weary spirits. They had cooked for one another. They had slept under the darkness made radiant by a billion stars. They talked of many things, punctuating their conversations with laughter and with silences. Always, just beneath the surface of their words, a tender cherishing flowed between them. He was the first man who ever listened to her story. She was the first woman who really saw him, penetrated his soul, and

[25] *Tomorrow Shall Be My Dancing Day*, a traditional English carol arranged by Nancy Grundahl, Music Director of Mayflower Congregational Community UCC, Minneapolis, Minnesota.

allowed him to be only himself. He was gentle and attentive as she halted and stammered to reconstruct the painful and shaming details of a woman caught in the maw of a violent and turbulent world. She rocked him on her breast when tears fell from his eyes, tears before the cruelty that people so casually inflicted upon one another.

In the last week violence had swirled around them, wrenched them apart, and engulfed them in a torturous nightmare. He had been seized, mocked, beaten, abandoned and executed. She was utterly bereft. There was no one to turn to, no one to help her understand, no one to heal this last and most devastating wound to her soul. His broken body had been removed from the desolate scene; it was lying in a cold tomb behind a great rock in a modest garden. His agony was over. Hers had just begun.

Choir Sings:

> Before Pilate the people me brought
> Where Barabbas had deliverance,
> They scourged me and set me at naught,
> Judged me to die to lead the dance.

> Sing O my love,
> Sing O my love, my love, my love,
> This I have done for my true love.

Voice One:

Her universe was collapsing, imploding, and sucking her into its vortex of nothingness. That the sun dared to rise today was a blasphemy against her grief. That everywhere people were rising from bed, washing, dressing, eating breakfast and preparing for another day, like any other day—this was incomprehensible to her. That she herself should live seemed a curse unimaginable; the days that stretched before her looked like so many gray walls of a barren prison.

But even here, in the garden of her grief, Life invaded her consciousness. Vivid memories of his smile, his smells, his touch rushed over her. The cooing of the pigeons overhead, the red and fragrant flowering of the pomegranates—these reminded her of poems they had recited to one another:

Voice Two:

"Come with me,
my love,
come away

For the long wet months are past,
the rains have fed the earth
and left it bright with blossoms

Birds wing in the low sky
dove and songbird are singing
in the open air above…

Come with me,
my love,
come away…

Until the day is over
and the shadows flee,
turn round, my lover,
Go quickly, and be
like deer or gazelles
in the cleft of the hills."[26]

Voice One:

But he would not turn toward her in the coolness of the morning. Her gazelle had fallen on the hill where men are executed. He would show himself no more.

She had come to the tomb, robes damp from dew still heavy on the bushes. Hers was the hypersensitivity of one who had not slept or eaten for days. Her face was terror-tensed as she stole quietly into the garden. She had come to tend his wounds and to touch him one last time. Silently she approached the tomb.

She brought oils and perfumes and soft cloths to prepare him properly for his burial. Where he had been flogged, she would breathe upon him the warmth of her breath. Where he had been punctured by nail and spear, she would tenderly kiss. There would be no magic in her caresses, she knew. Her ministrations would not restore life to him. This was necessary for her. She knew no other way to say good-bye.

---

[26] Marcia Falk. *The Song of Song: A New Translation and Interpretation*, 1990, from poems 9 & 12, (Song of Songs 2: 11-17).

Voice Two:

The last few days have been hell for them. His body lay two hours on the street where he had fallen. No one thought to cover it. No one knelt beside him. No one held his hand or head or offered a prayer. The loud and impersonal staccato of police radios, the roaring engine of a passing car, the distant wailing of an ambulance siren—these noises masked the awful silence into which Torrey Milon had descended. Squad cars parked obliquely; their flashing lights swept the street. Uniformed officers paced nervously this way and that. A news photographer bent awkwardly, trying to get the best angle of this scene. Neighbors gathered, but were kept at a distance.

Another gun, another bullet, another fifteen-year-old lay dead in the streets. A good kid, we are told, a high school freshman, a good student, the son and brother, the nephew and cousin of a loving family. He was biking home from the community center when he was shot. No obvious reason has emerged: Though his slaying might be "gang-related", family, friends and neighbors who knew him deny vehemently that he was a member of any gang. (And what difference would it make?)

Choir Sings:

Then on the cross hanged was I,
Where a spear to my heart did glance,
There issued forth both water and blood
To call my true love to the dance.

Voice Two:

For his family especially, and for everyone who cares about children, this killing was a senseless and brutal outrage. Violence and cruelty swirl around all children today, wherever they live, whatever the color of their skin. For the family and friends of Torrey Milon, anguish, grief and the fearful question of "Why?" make Holy Week especially painful, and Easter especially problematic. The sting of death is all too real. The victory of the grave is indisputable.

Voice One:

Melissa sat in her wheel chair, surrounded by other patients of the nursing home. Blue and white crepe paper and balloons hung from the ceiling. Those who were able sang "Happy Birthday" to this100-year-old lady whose memory is quite good and who understands her situation. Tears trickled down her cheek as she blew on candles standing askew on a white sheet cake. These were tears of memory. Her mother and father, her eight brothers and sisters, her husband and four children and countless friends all had died before her. She felt very much alone. "Nobody wants to be a burden," she once said, "but I've got nobody to be a burden on."

Voice Two:

Between Good Friday and Easter, according to tradition, Jesus himself descended into hell. It was not enough that he took on human flesh and human suffering. It was not enough that he immersed himself in our common life, experienced our pain, and shared our desperation. Tradi-

tion tells us that he entered hell itself, the last and final
citadel of negativity. He entered even hell to bring a message
of hope to those who had no hope, and transformation to
those who were despairing.

   Mary Magdalene, the Milons, and Melissa all know the
reality of hell. For Easter to have real meaning, more than
death must be conquered. The power of hell itself finally
must be vanquished.

Voice One:

   Nikolai Berdyaev was a Russian expatriate and one of
the most profound thinkers of our age. In his book, *The*
Destiny of Man, he declares that hell is real but it has no
objective existence. Hell as a place "is illusory, phantasma-
gorical and unreal, but it describes the greatest psycholog-
ical subjective reality for the individual." Hell, he writes, is
a denial of Eternity. It represents the loss of possibility, the
refusal of hope. Hell persists in our inability to love, in our
denial of the spirit, in the fragmentation of our personalities, and in our experience of absolute loneliness. Hell is
being shut up in self-centered suffering, never being able
to escape from self-centered agony.

   Hell is not the result of God's action upon our souls.
Rather, it is the soul's inability to open itself to God's influence. To Berdyaev "the horror of hell is not that God's
judgment is stern and implacable. God is mercy and
love, and to give one's fate to God is to overcome horror.
The horror is to have our fate in our own hands. It is not
what God will do to us that is terrible, but what we do to
ourselves."

Choir Sings:

> Then down to hell I took my way,
> For my true love's deliverance,
> Then rose again on the third day
> Up to my true love and the dance.

Voice One:

Václav Havel lamented that "the shocks of recent history... have led people to lose faith in the future, in the possibility of setting public affairs aright, in the meaning of a struggle for truth or justice...(We) succumb to apathy and indifference toward suprapersonal values and other people, to spiritual passivity and depression."[27] We know we are in hell when we must medicate our angst. When we seek to lose ourselves in the crowds. When we "zone out" before the television. When we "shop till we drop." When we join the ranks of the unfeeling.

Voice Two:

Despair may drain our energy, but it makes few demands. Grieving is not pleasant, but at least it is familiar. Many of us are more content to live lives of "quiet desperation" than to discover the truth about our world and ourselves. Is there any way out? All of God's action in the world is directed toward freeing us from hell. "The rise of hope," Berdyaev writes, "is the way out of hell."

---

[27] Václav Havel, "The Power of the Powerless", Reprinted in *The American Dissident*, 1978.

Voice One:

Many people have a Disneyesque understanding of Easter: Death does its worse. Jesus rises triumphantly. Everybody lives happily ever after. There is a problem with this view. In real life, even after Easter, death continues to hack its way through our world. It fells the just and the unjust with a callous disregard to station or situation. It takes away Torrey Milon at the threshold of his life, while it leaves Melissa to languish in her sorrow. The power of the Citadel of Negativity extends from first century Jerusalem to twentieth century Hebron, from a Samaritan hostel to a modern hospital room, and from Simon Peter's living room to your living room, and mine.

I suggest to you that Easter is not about happy endings. Religion is not about painless living. Faith is not about getting what we want. Rather, Easter provides the basis for us to make a bold assertion of hope when there is no reason to hope. Religion provides us with the purpose for living when living itself is painful. Faith enables us to give up what we want most desperately, trusting that God already knows and provides for our deepest and truest needs.

Easter testifies to our experience that there comes into our private anguish a Presence who is capable of transforming our minds, calming our hearts and refreshing our spirits. Into our social despair comes One who can transform our communities and our world. Even in the depths of hell itself, Christ ceaselessly strives to set us free from the heavy chains of negativity that pull us toward non-being. Even when we have no energy for Life, Life summons us anew. We can believe (and we must), wrote Berdyaev, that "the power of hell has been vanquished by Christ, and the final word belongs to God." This faith (and perhaps only this faith) has the power to change the world.

Voice Two:

Virginia Satir, a pioneer in family therapy, once said that when grief comes knocking at our doors, we resist it with all our might. We fear the loss, the pain. Instead, we might open the door and inquire, "What is your message for me?"

Annie Dillard tells us what we might find:

"In the deep are the violence and terror of which psychology has warned us. But if you ride these monsters deeper down, if you drop with them farther over the world's rim, you find what our sciences cannot locate or name, the substrate, the ocean or matrix or ether which buoys the rest, which gives goodness its power for goodness, and evil its power for evil, the unified field, our complex and inexplicable caring for one another, and for our life together."[28]

This is another way of saying what Berdyaev said. At the center of all reality is a transforming Love. Our "complex and inexplicable caring for one another and for our life together" is the firm foundation upon which we may confidently build a life. It is a core affirmation of the human personality on which all community is based. It contains within it the power to change our mourning into

[28] Annie Dillard, *Teaching a Stone to Talk*, 1988.

dancing, and our fears into joyous affirmations. "Weeping may endure for the night," exclaims the Psalmist, "but joy comes in the morning."[29]

Voice One:

If we truly believed in God's desire and ability to deliver us all from hell, could we even hear of Melissa's story, or Torrey's, without bolting into action? Could we ever be content with our own limited horizons or frozen hearts?

Voice Two:

Easter speaks to the deepest levels of our personality. It invites us to "ride these monsters deeper down" through layers of fear and confusion, fragmentation and death. It promises that we are not alone, and that out of the depths we will emerge with new life and power, new hope and energy.

Voice One:

Although Melissa's tears were tears of longing for those who had gone before her, and for her own deep loneliness, they also were tears of joy. She was happy for the people now in her life who listened to her stories, who absolved her of her guilt, who enjoyed her continuing life with them. Her grief was real, but so was her gratitude for the countless tender moments she had shared with her loved ones and for her very real contributions to the life of those around her. She knew in her heart that she did not live in vain. In this nursing home, she said with a wink,

[29] Psalm 30:5 (American King James Version).

she found "a whole new bunch of people she could be a burden on."

Voice Two:

At the site where Torrey Milon died, a neighbor erected a wooden cross. He painted on it the words, "Be With God," and also "Please, we must stop killing each other." The traffic has been steady at this little cross in the center of a struggling neighborhood. Kids and adults have stopped, and bus drivers, police officers and total strangers. Figurines and flowers have been placed by the cross, and messages that say, "We miss you," and "I love you," and "God bless you."

The neighbor who placed the cross is Charles Steen, a burly newspaper press operator who also bakes cookies for neighbors, kids, cops and firefighters. "I keep thinking that this is my fault and your fault," he said. "We got caught up in having the nicer car, the better job, and we've forgotten the important things. Kids like Torrey are paying the price for our neglect. I had to do something. I didn't want people to just see bloodstains on the street where that boy had died." The world needs less rage and more goodies, he believes.

"The answer is not more jails, more cops," he said. "The answer is more chocolate chip cookies." The answer is to keep gymnasiums open late at night so kids have constructive places to go. The answer is to hire people to teach kids skills such as how to bake cookies or play musical instruments. Maybe Charles and Susan Steen, and people like them, will begin to lead us from the hell of random violence,

and point us to the important things, "the inexplicable caring for one another and for our life together."[30]

Voice One:

Bill Holm, in his collection of poems called *The Dead Get By With Everything*, wrote:

"Someone dancing inside us
has learned only a few steps:
the 'Do-Your-Work' in 4/4 time,
and the 'What-Do-You-Expect' waltz.
He hasn't noticed yet the woman
standing away from the lamp,
the one with black eyes
who knows the rumba
and strange steps in jumpy
rhythms from the mountains of Bulgaria.
If they dance together,
something unexpected will happen.
If they don't, the next world
will be a lot like this one."

Christ invites us to a dance. It is a dance of Love. If we accept, something unexpected almost certainly will happen.

Choir Sings:

Then up to heaven I did ascend
Where now I dwell in sure substance,
On the right hand of God that all
May come unto the general dance.

---

[30] *Minneapolis Star Tribune,* March 21 & 24, 1994.

Sing O my love,
Sing O my love, my love, my love,
This I have done for my true love.

Voice Two:

*Easter presents us with this invitation. Do we hold fast
to our familiar grief and fear, our dreams for how things
should be? Or, even in the midst of much suffering and
tragedy, can we let go of them? Can we abandon our hope
for a cure or a fix, in order to know real healing? Can we
stop trying to hold together the fragments of our lives, so
that we might come to know the real wholeness of our
personalities? Can we "ride these monsters deeper down" to
the liberating core?*

Voice One:

Mary Magdalene approached the tomb, wide-eyed
with bewilderment. The huge stone that she imagined
would be such a problem had been rolled from the entrance. Inside, bloody linens were neatly folded at the
foot of the crypt; the tomb itself was empty. Her grief
turned into panic. Would she not even be able to treat his
wounds, cleanse his body, and soothe her troubled spirit?
She saw the gardener looking at her. She froze with fear.
Then she timidly asked him, "I am looking for the body
of Jesus of Nazareth. They laid him in this tomb. But he is
not here. Do you know where they have taken him?" She
felt like fainting as she waited for his answer. It seemed an
eternity that she waited, teetering forever between hope

and despair. Then came his voice, so familiar and reassuring. "Mary," he said. And she knew Easter in her heart.

After the earthquake

"From noon on, darkness came over the whole land until three in the afternoon. And about three o'clock Jesus cried with a loud voice, 'Eli, Eli, lema sabachthani?' that is, 'My God, my God, why have you forsaken me?' When some of the bystanders heard it, they said, 'This man is calling for Elijah.' At once one of them ran and got a sponge, filled it with sour wine, put it on a stick, and gave it to him to drink. But the others said, 'Wait; let us see whether Elijah will come to save him.' Then Jesus cried again with a loud voice and breathed his last. At that moment the curtain of the temple was torn in two, from top to bottom. The earth shook, and the rocks were split." Matthew 27: 45-51

"After the Sabbath, as the first day of the week was dawning, Mary Magdalene and the other Mary went to see the tomb. And suddenly there was a great earthquake; for an angel of the Lord, descending from heaven, came and rolled back the stone and sat on it. His appearance was like lightning and his clothing white as snow. For fear of him the guards shook and became like dead men. But the angel said to the women, 'Do not be afraid; I know that you are looking for Jesus who was crucified. He is not here; for he has been raised, as he said. Come, see the place where he lay. Then go quickly and tell his disciples, He has been raised from the dead, and indeed he is going ahead of you to Galilee; there you will see him. This is my message for you.'" Matthew 28:1-7

An earthquake struck the crowded city at the height of Pesach celebrations. Homes were lying in ruins. Streets were impassable. Wells were polluted. The immense curtains of the Temple had been rent asunder. Graves opened in a macabre tango of death with life. The high-pitched keening of women's voices ascended from every quarter of the city.

People were beginning to move about. With subdued voices they talked together, assessed the damage and began repairs. Soldiers in battle dress warily patrolled the streets. A tense and distrustful mood lay upon Yeru-Sha-lom—this city that eternally longs for peace. No one heard the birds singing overhead. It was an angry city just now. A potential violence far greater than any earthquake lay just below the surface.

In was not unlike many cities in the world today, including especially present-day Jerusalem and Ramallah. The disorientation of those quake-shaken survivors of Yeru-Shalom finds an answering echo in the lives of all who have been traumatized by cataclysm. The shifting of the earth beneath our feet, our lingering vulnerability and our aching losses—all these we share with our ancient counterparts.

The young rabbi and prophet, Yeshua of Nazareth, had come to celebrate the first night of Pesach with his disciples. He had been betrayed, arrested, tried, tortured and sentenced to his death—all in a single night. He died the next day—a cruel death by crucifixion—just before Shabbat began, this Sabbath in the Holy Land. His body was removed from the cross and hurriedly buried in a borrowed tomb. It lay there until now, the third day of Passover.

People had been stunned by this outrageous injustice, the unspeakable obscenity of this violence against so innocent a young rabbi, just as we are stunned today by the coldhearted acts of suicide bombers and ruthless military retaliation. Some quietly closed their doors and shutters out of fear or grief. Others furtively began to sharpen their swords. Such heavy-handed oppression guaranteed that rebellions and uprisings would continue for another forty years, until finally the Romans profaned and destroyed the Temple itself, and Hebrew Zealots chose suicide over subjugation at Massada—for themselves and the women and children who were with them. Until the Roman empire itself collapsed from the internal corrosion of corruption, greed and the misjudging of the source of ultimate power.

As the sun climbed over the beleaguered community, stark, broken, skeletal remains of fallen buildings were emerging from darkness. The warmth of the rising sun dispelled the cold dampness of the night's air. It began its quiet work of healing the heaviness in their hearts. In spite of their conflicted grief and anger, they welcomed its warmth upon their flesh. As they started to organize the slow hard work of reconstructing their city, their psyches too began the inevitable work of adjusting to the new reality.

The dull hues of nearby stone and streets, the subtle greens of the few surrounding trees, the splotches of bright color on birds' wings and wagon wheels – these became their healers. The chattering of birds and children pushed back the edge of their pain, and made space for the return of Life.

In the city there was a garden among the tombs. Within it the lifeless body of the young teacher had been placed. Now two close friends came to say their farewells. It was dangerous for them to do so; he had been marked and executed as traitor to the "Peace of Rome"—that bloody and soulless Pax maintained by force of arms. But they came anyway—weeping and fearful—because there was no other place on earth for them now. Here by the dead body of their beloved friend they would remain until …until…until it was time for them to go.

In Jesus they had glimpsed the hidden strength of true humility. They had seen how love could overcome fear. He gave them Life when death and emptiness threatened. From him they learned that nothing intrinsically good is ever lost. It endures. It persists. It finds new expressions. God is Love; that which love reveals must be eternal. He taught them to honor the Sacred within themselves so that they could honor it within others and all creation. He gave them confidence. Who would teach them now?

Upon entering the garden they were astonished. The change in the atmosphere was palpable. Their tension and anger dissipated. It was as though they had passed through a veil into another world. The heaviness in their bodies fell from them. Their hearts became brighter and their steps more eager. They looked at each other with wonder.

Without understanding, they continued to move forward. The despair that had been tearing at their hearts was lifting. They found themselves—quite unexpectedly—in a place of amazing tranquility. Time stood still. Birds sang in the branches above them. Only the trailing of their garments against the shrubs disturbed the expectant hush they were experiencing.

Hesitantly they approached his tomb. Here in death's dust lay the one whom they cherished most in life. Here lay gentleness and laughter, courage and compassion. Here lay truth. Here lay beauty. Here lay love's greatest teacher. But as they approached the grave it dawned upon them—as surely as the sun had dawned in the early morning sky—that this grieving was wrong, terribly wrong.

As if to punctuate their poignant reflections, a second tremor shook the garden itself. The ground beneath them shifted as they approached the tomb. They stumbled. The earth shuddered and the great rock rolled from the entrance. A messenger of God proclaimed to them the unthinkable, that Jesus was not dead but raised, not in the tomb but going before them into Galilee. The women were stunned.

With the two Marys we also have come to this garden today. We too are perplexed. We live in a world of broken lives and broken promises, vain hopes and vanished dreams. We have seen too many endings, attended too many funerals. What does this mean to us?

Everywhere we look enemies are locked in escalating spirals of pain. Violence is answered with violence in ascending cycles of destruction. We know fear. Catastrophes destroy much that we cherish. Emotional eruptions wreak havoc in our families. We endure pain and loss —too often without any sense of purpose or redemption. Our losses are real and our suffering is profound. We come thinking that our healing begins here and radiates from this now empty tomb.

But the three synoptic gospels practically scream at us that the living Christ will not be found here, not among the flowers, not in any mausoleum. He is alive. He goes before us into Galilee. He goes before us into the broken and shattered world from which we came. He goes before us into our homes and work settings, where we study and where we play. In Christ, God is overcoming death's oppression. We cannot pay homage here. We should not re-bury him in shrines and sacred places. To celebrate Easter we must leave the sanctuary and follow where he leads. We must seek Him in the places of greatest need. We must not memorialize him but serve him, not with spices and wrapping cloths but with our very lives.

Even after the earthquake Life persists. It will not be denied. As surely as the sun rises to warm and soothe our flesh after a cold damp night, as surely as the shadows flee before its advancing light, just as surely God's grace advances into the darkest places of our distress. As surely as the rising sun stirs up the song of creation within the breasts of the birds, it awakens the song of re-creation within us. We do not know how this happens, but that it happens we testify.

Today is the first day of resurrection for us. Today is the first day of God's new creation. Today Christ challenges the destructive powers around us. He goes before us even now. He quietly transforms and redeems our most sordid and desolate situations. Though demonic forces may appear to have the upper hand, though Wrong sits enthroned in capitals and boardrooms around the globe, though life's most cherished values seem crushed and lying in the dust, even now Christ goes before us. In Him God is still speaking. God is calling us to become a people of the resurrection, to proclaim a gospel of grace, and to restore a broken world to wholeness.

From garden to garden

"When the Sabbath was over, Mary Magdalene, and Mary the mother of James, and Salome bought spices, so that they might go and anoint him. And very early on the first day of the week, when the sun had risen, they went to the tomb. They had been saying to one another, 'Who will roll away the stone for us from the entrance to the tomb?' When they looked up, they saw that the stone, which was very large, had already been rolled back. As they entered the tomb, they saw a young man, dressed in a white robe, sitting on the right side; and they were alarmed. But he said to them, 'Do not be alarmed; you are looking for Jesus of Nazareth, who was crucified. He has been raised; he is not here. Look, there is the place they laid him. But go, tell his disciples and Peter that he is going ahead of you to Galilee; there you will see him, just as he told you.' So they went out and fled from the tomb, for terror and amazement had seized them; and they said nothing to anyone, for they were afraid." Mark 16:1-8

The sun was setting and the Sabbath was about to begin. A small group of his closet friends scrambled madly to lower the cross. They removed the spikes. They lifted his bloodied and lifeless body. In a tortured rush they hauled it down the road from Golgotha to a quickly borrowed tomb. Men and women together—we cannot see their faces. Were they weeping, or were they grimly silent? What they had witnessed in the previous 24 hours defies description and, anyway, is better left unsaid. But their memories of it would haunt them forever. Exhaustion, despair, rage, grief and helplessness churned in their hearts.

Though acting together, each one felt profoundly alone. The darkness of night enveloped them. By torchlight, under the intimidating scowls of Roman soldiers, they interred his body hastily, without ritual or ceremony. Then they turned away. They could hear the heavy stone rolling in its trough until it closed the tomb completely. They hurried to their homes. It was Shabbat; nothing more was permitted.

Imagine them, that first Good Friday evening. Did the women light the Sabbath candles? Did anyone break bread or eat? Did they talk, or sing, or weep or pray for comfort? We do not know. Their doors and windows are closed to us, and their hearts shut up in pain.

Did they sleep at all, that first "Good" Friday night? The women, at least, knew what to do next. When the Sabbath was over, they gathered soap, spices and ointments. They collected cloth appropriate for wrapping a body, and they waited for the dawn. As the sun rose they met outside and quietly carried their bundles toward the place where Jesus lay. They were intent to honor him in death as he had been dishonored in life, to wash and anoint his body, to tend his wounds, and to consign him to the loving care of the Holy One of Israel. They approached the garden in which the borrowed tomb was situated. They hoped and believed that the armed guards would open the grave long enough for them to perform these final obligations.

They approached the garden silently—"while the dew was still on the roses" a later hymn writer would imagine. As the first birds began to chirp and sing, they were comforted in spite of themselves. Sunlight began to warm their bodies and dispel the gloominess in their hearts. They were engulfed by the colors of this well-tended garden. Smells of flowers, mulch and freshly broken earth awakened and uplifted their spirits in spite of their heavy grief. As they approached the tomb, it seemed that nature itself would join with them in this last and loving tribute.

Why do we love gardens so much? From quaint English gardens to the manicured expanse of Versailles, from austere Zen gardens to the grandeur of the Alhambra, from the hanging gardens of ancient Mesopotamia to the terrariums we create in our classrooms—people in many cultures and in many lands love these oases of loveliness. Gardens calm us, comfort us, uplift us, and inspire us. Sometimes nothing is more healing that a few hours working or walking in our gardens.

Scripture tells us that God was first of all a gardener. The first chapters of Genesis show God designing and creating a delicately balanced planetary garden. Within this creation God placed a special garden for humankind. Scripture calls it Eden; some have called it Paradise. God's first call to humanity was to enjoy the garden. Created in God's image, our first vocations were to be gardeners. The journey to our full humanity begins in a garden. When we walk or work in our gardens today, we touch one of the deepest roots of our collective being. We remember or imagine a time when we were innocent, safe and cared for. These unconscious associations penetrated the hearts of the women on that first Easter morning, and lightened their burden as they approached the tomb.

If gardens evoke a faint recollection of Paradise, it is, sadly, the recollection of a paradise lost. For reasons that remain mysterious, humanity overreached its original vocation, was cast out and barred from returning. According to the story, our ancient ancestors were forced to leave the garden in shame. The first murder occurred between brothers shortly thereafter. Eve wept for her sons, as the women of Ramah wept for their murdered children when Jesus was born.[31] As these women were weeping now.

Jesus knew about gardens. Like us, he went to gardens to pray, to weigh the great issues in his life and to be led to great decisions. As his hour approached, he retreated to the garden of Gethsemane. He went there to face the truth about himself and his vocation. In Gethsemane he engaged in a fierce struggle with his God. It has been said that in Gethsemane he encountered again his demons, his tempters. In Gethsemane, finally, he found clarity. Clarity, yes, but not comfort. In Gethsemane, too, he was betrayed, arrested, bound and taken away. If Eden was the

---

[31] Genesis 4 / Jeremiah 31: 15 / Matthew 2: 16-18.

garden where innocence was lost, Gethsemane was the garden where it was betrayed.

On this day, these women entered a different garden. Eden was but a shadowy memory. Gethsemane was shrouded in darkness. This garden contained the lifeless body of the One who came to give Life. This was the garden of ultimate defeat, the garden of eternal grieving, of endless lament, of the solemn loss of hope itself. They had come only to wash the body.

They dragged their heavy hearts to the doorway of the tomb. But they were startled as they approached. The stone had been removed. In their confusion they looked inside; the body was gone. Only the bloodied burial sheet remained. And a strangely beautiful stranger. When they asked about the body, they were greeted with a riddle. "Why do you look for the living among the dead?"

Why, indeed? Do you remember *The Secret Garden*? One hundred years ago Frances Hodgson Burnett wrote what was to become a classic of children's literature. Do you remember the story? The young Mary Leonard lost everyone who loved her, and whom she had loved, to the disease of cholera. She was sent from India to live on the Yorkshire estate of her morose and brooding uncle, Archibald. But Archibald himself was mired in unhealed grief for his beloved wife, Lily. His dying son, Colin, was condemned to live his brief life within the darkly melancholic confines of the 100-room estate.

Everywhere there was death and morbidity, hopelessness and despair. But one day Mary found a walled garden. It had been Lily's, and it had been abandoned and locked since Lily's death. Like the estate itself, like the lives of nearly everyone around her, the garden seemed lifeless and dead. But given her indomitable spirit, hers and that of a Yorkshire neighbor, they brought it back to life. Soon plants and flowers began to blossom. Birds returned. It became a garden of healing and redemption. In this garden Mary recovered, Colin learned to walk, and even Archibald emerged from the prison of his grief. The secret garden was created as a place of love and delight. Then it became the embodiment of deep, fierce, consuming, unhealed grief. With Mary's touch it became a place of recovery, discovery, regeneration and healing. The whole story is about "wick." Wick in Yorkshire dialect means "life" or "alive." "Wick" exists within the dryness and apparent lifelessness of plants; it enables them to return to vitality in due season. "Wick"—Life—is the magic of the universe, and it is more powerful than all the forces of death and despair that are arrayed against it.

"Why do you look for the living among the dead?" Why do we look for "wick" among the straw? Physically exhausted and spiritually shattered, these women tried to understand. "Not here?" they thought? "Living?" they asked. How can this be? But as the meaning began to sink in, they became giddy with wonder. The garden of defeat had been turned into the Garden of Resurrection.

Centuries later an Orthodox priest would capture the paradox and wonder of this moment:

"No one can put together what has crumbled into dust, but Thou canst restore a conscience turned to ashes. Thou canst restore to its former beauty a soul lost and without hope. With Thee there is nothing that cannot be redeemed. Thou art love; Thou art Creator and Redeemer. We praise Thee, singing: Alleluia!"[32]

The Garden of Easter became a new Eden. Christ opened its gates to us and invites us to return. This is the first day of the week as scripture asserts, but it is much, much more: Today is the first day of a new creation.

Scripture speaks of at least one more garden. In the Book of Revelation, John tells a vision of the new creation. He sees a "New Jerusalem" descending from the heavens at the end of time. It is a new city, and in it he sees all the nations of the earth gathered in peace. Each one "brings its glory" to the city. In the New Jerusalem there are no temples to be seen anywhere. No synagogues, no church-

---

[32] "Kontakian 10" from *The Akathist Hymn: "Glory to God for All Things* attributed to Protopresbyter Gregory Petrov who wrote it shortly before his death in a Stalinist camp in the Gulag in 1940. It was set to music by John Tavener in 1994.

es, no gurdwaras, no mosques—for the energy of God is unveiled. In the center of this city flows a river of crystal clear water, and along its banks on both sides is a garden. In the garden are trees that bear many kinds of fruit simultaneously; the leaves of these trees are used for the healing of nations. In this garden and in this city there is no weeping, no sadness, no depression, no anger, no violence, no warfare, and no exploitation. This is the garden and the city toward which all history is moving.[33]

We live, sometimes, within the garden. When we do, we see and experience the translucent beauty of all creation. Joy is all around us, and promise.

But more often like the disciples—women and men— we live between gardens. Their lives unfolded in the market place, the courts, the shops, and on the sea. We live in a crowded public square, immersed in a strident and partisan cacophony. In these "between times" it is good to remember Eden and to work toward the New Jerusalem. It is good to remember the beauty we have experienced and to anticipate the beauty we have been promised.

As human beings, we are created for life in the garden. In the Garden of Creation our journey began. In the Garden of Paradise our lives shall fully blossom. But between these gardens we are called to be nurturers of "wick"

---

[33] Revelation 21

where there appears to be no life, and of hope where hopelessness endures. Every day is an Easter Day for us if we open our eyes, every day a new creation. Every day with the living Christ makes of our lives the most beautiful "secret gardens" of the soul.

The art of Easter[34]

For some ministers, Easter sermons are difficult to write. I was having trouble with mine when a seminary classmate dropped by.

"What's the matter with you?" Peter inquired.

"My yearly attack of Easter anxiety. Occupational hazard, I suppose."

"You're allergic to lilies?"

"Beside that! It's not that I don't believe in resurrection. I have trouble talking about that one." He sat down and I poured him a cup of coffee.

"*Grave* doubts, I gather."

"Oh Peter! Easter is the celebration of new life. We experience resurrection with the coming of every spring, the birth of a child, or the rebirth of a person who has lost all hope. People find it even when confronted with the certainty of their own mortality.

"It is also a rite of spring," I continued, "a vestige of ancient fertility cults. For example, what creature on earth is thought to be the most prolific? The rabbit—the Easter bunny. And what about all those colored eggs—perfect symbols of new life. The shell is like a tomb and…"

"Christ is like a baby chick? Come on! A butterfly breaks out of its chrysalis too, but kids aren't eating chocolate cocoons."

[34] "Easter Concerns the Real Earth," *The Congregationalist*, April 1974.

"Of course not," I muttered. "It's deeper than this."

"Budd, didn't Susan Sontag once write that 'real art has the capacity to make us nervous'?"[35]

"I think so. People are frightened by today's art. It can be understood on so many different levels. It suggests so many possibilities."

"Good art is usually ambiguous."

"What are you getting at?"

"Perhaps your anxiety is rooted in the ambiguous nature of the Easter celebration itself. When we speak of Easter, maybe we're speaking of our collective art, and not of our history."

"I don't understand."

"Let's pretend, Budd, that this is the third century CE. A friend takes you to church. You listen to the celebrant recount many divine blessings before he invites you to the table of the Lord. He then distributes the bread and wine according to a certain formula. In what church are you worshipping?"

"Congregational?"

"No. This is real wine. You might have been attending the worship of the Lord Serapis—an Egyptian deity."

"Let's try it again."

[35] Susan Sontag, *Against Interpretation*, 1964.

"This time my fiancée describes her religion—its stately processions, its tonsured priests, its matins and vespers, its baptisms and holy water, its solemn ritual, its jeweled images of the Mother of God. About what faith is she conversing?"

"I would guess Roman Catholic, or Orthodox, or maybe the Episcopalians are high."

"Wrong again. She would have been discussing the cult of Isis, another Egyptian deity who was immensely popular in the ancient world.

"Suppose," Peter continued, "that you hear of a widespread faith whose founder is reputed to have said, 'Lift the stone and I am there; cleave the wood and I am there.' One of its most distinguished teachers may have taught a doctrine of the soul's re-incarnation in successive world periods. Which religion is this?"

"Dare I answer?"

"Actually, this is Christianity. You recognized the quote from the recently discovered Gospel According to Thomas. The teacher, of course, was Origen, one of the foremost theologians in the early church."

"He was condemned as a heretic."

"Yes, but two centuries after he died!"

"Let me turn the tables," I said. Suppose another of our classmates enlightens us at dinner about a religion whose founder may have been a reformer within an older religion. Little is known of his life, but his image appears frequently in the catacombs where he is often depicted as the Good Shepherd.

"He is called the son of God. Some claim that he died, descended into Hades and was resurrected. His followers place great stress on a book of holy writings. They worship a creator-god. They believe a story about the origin of humanity that includes an explicit doctrine of original 'sin' —uncommon at the time. They anticipate a future life in which the individual soul will find either bliss or punishment.

"The death of the prophet is reenacted regularly in a ritual meal during which his 'body' is broken and consumed. What is it?"

"Sounds Christian to me, but I know it isn't," Peter replied.

"It isn't. This is the Orphic religion. The prophet-teacher-god is Orpheus."

"When I was in Berlin I saw a hematite amulet dating from the third century. It shows a human figure nailed to a cross. And the inscription? 'Orpheus Bakkikos'!"

"And we both know of a Fourth Century Christian church in Aquileia, Peter, twenty-two miles northwest of Trieste, which was built early in the fourth century. Professor Samuel Laeuchli[36] of Temple University described it to us when we were at Princeton. Remember? In its mosaic pavements there is a portrait of Christ as

---

[36] Samuel Laeuchli is the author of *Religion and Art in Conflict*, 1980.

the good shepherd—an allusion to David, no doubt. But what he holds in his hand is most significant. It is the Orphic flute."

"The Dionysian flute," Peter interrupted. "It probably alludes to all three—Christ, David and Orpheus! We celebrate Easter in the spring, no doubt, because of Passover. But I suggest that it is more than that. We also must recognize the impact of these pagan religions on the infant Christian church. As a sub-sect of the Dionysian religion, the Orphic cult was a major fertility cult in that ancient environment."

"Then the similarities are not accidental? Our faith really is a synthesis!"

"Absolutely," he exclaimed. "These religions provided the framework within which our faith came into being. Even the 'Christ' we worship retains attributes from these earlier sources."

"Is that all? I was expecting more."

"Mark, Matthew, Luke and John were not journalists. They were artists, shaping a synthesis from the religious materials in their world—Jewish and pagan themes in particular."

"In other words, they were more akin to James Joyce than to James Reston[37]?"

"Precisely, although both of your examples indulge

---

[37] A popular American journalist and award-winning columnist for *The New York Times*.

themselves in fantasy. The evangelists did not have our criteria for truth. They were not scientists. They would find unintelligible today's debates about statistical probabilities of virgin births, resurrections or anything else. They were artists. By reflecting the ancient world through the new perspective of the Christian faith, they gave religion a new depth and a new dimension."

"So you think they made the whole thing up?"

"I didn't say that. But one English scholar, G. A. Wells, argues cogently that Christianity could have emerged without any single human founder.[38] The conditions were right. You've read enough of Sir James Fraser's classic, *The Golden Bough*, to know how widespread were the notions of a dying god and resurrection."

"Yes," I added. "I also believe that much of the gospel material was shaped to conform to the themes and prophecies of the Hebrew Bible."

"This leads me to think, Budd, that the early Christians didn't read these narratives as we do. They experienced them. The church was composed of converts from the religions of Moses, Mithra, Orpheus, Osiris, Isis and others. It must have been enriched by this interpenetration of such diverse understandings and practices."

"You say that these early believers 'experienced' the

[38] G. H. Wells, *The Jesus of the Early Christians*, 1971.

gospels. Well, I know something of how I feel when I 'experience' Joyce's *Ulysses*.[39] How did they experience the Easter narratives?"

"Tell me briefly of your reactions to Joyce's novel."

"It's a difficult book. I can't say that I completely understand it, but I react on several levels. There's the me who is curious about what really happened in Dublin in early June, 1904. That's the scholarly reaction, I suppose. There's the me who simply enjoys being overwhelmed by the text, by the occasional beauty or frightfulness of his imagery. There's the playful me who tries to discover the hidden relationships throughout the book. There's the me who is slightly scandalized by the vulgarities. And, of course, there's the me who identifies with Bloom in his predicament. Probably there are a dozen more me's who read the book as well."

"You're good! That's really excellent, Budd. The third century Christian may have come to his gospels in the same way. Allow me to digress, and it will become plain.

"When a Christian joined the fellowship, he (or she) first underwent rigorous instruction. On Easter Eve, he was brought to the church in a simple white gown. A priest exorcised evil spirits from around him as he entered. He then faced west and renounced his 'pact with Hades.' He faced east and announced his allegiance to

---

[39] James Joyce, *Ulysses*, originally published in 1922.

Christ. He was made to kneel on an animal skin and spent the night in vigil.

"Before dawn, he was stripped of his robe and taken, naked, to the baptismal pool. There he was completely immersed. This signified that he had 'died' with Christ and was buried—under water. When he emerged, he symbolically 'rose' with Christ. His first words were, 'Christ is risen.'

"The initiate was then given a new white linen robe, symbolizing the garment of Christ after the transfiguration. He was, symbolically at least, a new person. Similar rites were practiced by other mystery religions at the time."

"That's bizarre, but it beats sprinkling."

"Listen carefully. Mark tells of a young man who was with Jesus in the garden. He fled at the time of Jesus' arrest. He wore only a linen cloth that was pulled from him, and he ran away naked (14: 51-52). Later in the same book the women who gathered at the tomb saw a young man within it who was clothed in 'a long white garment' and who announced the resurrection (16: 5). Some scholars believe it is meant to be the same person.

"That story may not have happened quite as it is depicted. Rather, the reader is supposed to make the connection, and to see himself as the young man in both narratives—at first a frightened Jesus groupie, and later a messenger of the resurrection."

"In other words, baptism is a symbolic participation in the suffering, death and resurrection of Christ."

"And the suffering, death and resurrection of Christ is an artistic way of expressing the believer's personal experience of transformation. Regardless of its roots in Jewish cult or pagan mystery religion, Easter celebrates the most fundamental of human experiences."

"I can understand that," I exclaimed. "As a country parson, I see it every day. I know of a colleague, for example, who believed that he was really ineffective in his ministry. He felt frustrated, trapped, unappreciated and useless. But another church saw a gift in him that his own people were blind to. As the new minister in that church, he has become a regular prophet in the pulpit and a keen, sensitive pastor in the counseling situation. He's a different person. That's resurrection."

"And I know of a case," Peter interrupted, "where the husband and the wife were literally destroying each other and their children too. For over a decade they maintained the semblance of married life. Eventually they recognized that the marriage had died somewhere along the way, and they've since gotten a divorce. Although the realization was crushing at the time, I am amazed at the personal transformation each has undergone. New strength has appeared, new identities have emerged. And the kids? They're not 'sadder but wiser.' They're happier and better somehow. They can experience life more deeply than they dared before."

"This has obvious social applications too. Out of the collapse of a decadent world rose a new civilization. Out of the religious oppression of the seventeenth century came the Mayflower. Out of Watergate…who knows?"

"But to believe in resurrection in this way means to accept suffering and death as well, does it not? For the phoenix to rise from its ashes, it must accept its baptism of fire."

ʹ"Yes. Easter concerns the real earth and not some never-never-land." I looked at my seed catalogs. "Sometimes a seed must 'die' to bring new life. To deny grief or pain, to resist the so-called negative aspects of life, is to prevent the possibility of transformation. Jesus is portrayed as willingly accepting the cross. Via crucis, via pacem. It is a difficult affirmation, this Easter business, but a necessary one."

"Then go ahead and celebrate these rites of spring. Immerse your congregation in the art of the Easter narratives. Color those eggs. Pass out chocolate cocoons. Proclaim the promises embedded in our common experiences.

"Easter is sheer, unadulterated possibility. It is Dionysian. It is Christian. It is even Joyce's Molly, rendering that unforgettable and unequivocal 'Yes!' to life."

For further reading you may wish to consult:

Jean Danielou. *The Bible and the Liturgy*. South Bend: University of Notre Dame Press, 1956

W. K. C. Gutherie. *Orpheus and Greek Religion*. New York: W.W. Norton F Co., 1966.

Robbin Scroggs and Kent I. Groff. "Baptism in Mark," T*he Journal of Biblical Literature*, December, 1973, pp.531-548.

Afterword: Befriending the storm

"They were filled with great awe, and said to one another,
'Who is this, that even the wind and the sea obey him?'"
Mark 4: 41

They braced themselves against the sides of the boat.
They held desperately to anything that would keep them
from being pulled into the vast and churning sea.
Their own sheer terror held them fast.
The sea lifted them toward exploding lightening
and then hurled them into the abyss—
their little craft a tiny speck in a raging vortex,
dipping and turning and swirling wildly out of control.

Their boat groaned beneath thunderous detonations
    overhead.
Blinding sheets of rain lashed and stung them,
driving them more deeply into their fear,
until there only was fear,
fear and darkness,
fear, saturating their souls more surely than
    torrential rain,
until they became their fear—
wincing eyes, clenched jaws, taut bodies,
and nothing more,
unable to control the storm, the boat,
or the pounding of their hearts.

One among them was sleeping,
asleep in the bow,
asleep though the cataclysm was upon them,

asleep though time itself was ending,
asleep though the sun was no more,
nor the moon, nor the stars,
but only wind, wind, wicked wind,
and rain,
and pelting darkness.

If they could awaken this one,
he would calm the turmoil.
If they could awaken the Master,
He would save them from this storm.

They cried out.
They cried above the cacophony of the vanishing universe.
Out of the place of deepest darkness they cried,
"O Master, hear us!
O Master, save us!"

The Master heard, and awakened.
Bracing himself against the rail, he stood.
He looked at the disciples,
and at the sea,
at the disciples,
and at the sea.

He spoke.
His voice was so tender,
so quiet, so filled with love
that only Love itself could hear it.

But they heard it,
though what they heard they could not say.
Whether with ears or hearts they did not know.
But they heard the center of calm
in the center of the voice—
this voice,
centered in something bigger than the boat,
bigger than the storm, bigger the sea;
this voice—
centered in something bigger even than the world itself
and all that dwells therein.

He engaged the storm.
He befriended it.
He listened, talked, communed.
The thunder rumbled rebelliously,
but its intensity subsided.
Lightening strikes became less ominous.

The rain became just that: only rain,
no longer the assassin bent upon
hurling them into oblivion.

Fierce winds gentled into breezes.
Shafts of sunlight pierced the deep darkness.
Their taut, clenched muscles loosened.
Fear released its constricting grasp of their hearts.

Would they return to the land of the living? They did
  not know.
Would they sit once more by the fires of the hearths of
  their homes?
Soothe the thirst of their parched throats with cups of
  honeyed mead?
Massage aching muscles with oils from flowers and
  olive trees?
Would they look again into the eyes of children,
or be stroked once more by a lover's fingers?
Whether they would live or die,
they could not say.

But they heard the calm
in the center of the voice
from the center of the world
and the sea was calmed,
and the sky was calmed,
and they were calmed.

When breaking storms obscure our vision,
when all that is dear or familiar disappears,
when our horizons vanish,
when our future is in jeopardy,
and we are trapped in a terrible "now,"
when our life
or our sanity
or our very existence

hangs by the thinnest of threads,
when life becomes so difficult that it seems unbearable,
when tragedies engulf us,
when fears overwhelm us,
when we see no light at all,
when we have no reason to keep going,
when we are weary of the struggle,
when we are scared out of our wits,
when we just want to die—
to whom or to what can we turn?
What enables us to continue?
What strengthens us to persist?
What braces us to carry on?

Ludwig von Beethoven, the eldest, survived his alcoholic
father who dissipated the family's inheritance, and the
death of his mother and four siblings in childhood.
Ludwig dropped out of school at the age of eleven and
at eighteen he was the chief financial support for the
family.

He became a performer whose virtuosity surpassed
even Mozart's. Critics acclaimed his brilliance and promise. But by his thirtieth birthday he was aware of an
encroaching deafness. For the rest of his life he saw a suc-
cession of doctors but none was able to help. His condition was permanent, incurable, untreatable,
progressive, and would eventually be total. As his hearing
declined, his playing deteriorated. He had to give it up

altogether. He struggled with depression and more than once he thought of suicide.

Yet he did not take his life. He did not abandon his music. He continued to compose long after his deafness was total. By 1819 he was conversing with others only through notebooks, but he also was writing music of exquisite beauty—music he would never hear. The profoundly moving Missa Solemnis, the stirring affirmation of the Ninth Symphony, the extraordinary loveliness of his String Quartets—all these he wrote out of the raging silence that engulfed him.

As his Ninth Symphony with its exultant 'Ode to Joy' was performed for the first time Beethoven sat in the front row. He attempted to follow the music with the score but became confused. At its conclusion he was completely unaware of the thunderous applause until one of the soloists came down to him and turned him to face the audience.

What sustained and encouraged him to go on in spite of his great loss? He came to know and trust the extraordinary reality of music only he could hear. When he rejected the option of suicide he wrote to a friend, "It seemed unthinkable for me to leave the world forever before I had produced all the music I felt I had been called to produce... ."

"All the music I had been called to produce... ." This music was his Master.

By 1910 rheumatoid arthritis had so crippled the French Impressionist painter, Jean-Auguste Renoir, that he could no longer walk. His pain was constant and intense. His hands were mere stubs; he no longer could hold a brush. In 1915 his son was severely wounded in the war. Shortly thereafter his wife died. By then he was confined to a wheel chair and unable to walk even a little distance.

Yet he had friends strap brushes to his hands and he painted. What did he paint? Pictures of gloom, anguish or despair? No.

He created vibrant paintings of delicacy and loveliness. To this day they reveal a 'joie de vivre;' they celebrate the intrinsic beauty of life's most mundane experiences. Still-lifes, street scenes and figure studies—they convey a delight which resided in his soul. At the center of his life was his enthrallment by beauty, and beauty calmed his desperate, swirling seas.

Helen Johnson was a member of our congregation for many years. An archeology of her accent would reveal all the places she had lived: Scotland, South Africa, New England, Georgia. In her long life she had known deep losses, and the need to go on alone. Her heart bore the scars of separation from loved ones in space and in time, in life, and through death. But we recognized in her something quite singular: a peace, a confidence, an assurance of the basic goodness of life.

Prayer was her art form and time the raw material from which she fashioned exquisite gifts of kindness—glimpses of grace for those who crossed her path. Like all of us, she had doubts and fears but at the center of her center there was her prayer, and at the center of her prayer there was the still, small voice of Love.

❀❀❀

The vast majority of humankind knows that reality is hard, that life is difficult, that suffering is

> *...so high, we can't get over it,*
> *so low, we can't get under it,*
> *so wide, we can't get around it,*
> *we gotta go through the door.*

Sometimes,
when we're caught in a hideous storm,
when our lives are engulfed by the tempest,
we have no alternative but to row on,
to go through the raging sea.

But—and here's the most important part—
we are not alone, never alone.
Within the little boat of every life the Master is with us,
    waiting.
The Master may take the form of a sublime music heard
    by no one else.
The Master may take the form of a vision of loveliness
    perceived by no one else.

The Master may come in the form of memories.
The Master may come in dreams.

The Master may meet us in our prayers and meditations.
The Master may come in the smile of a stranger,
in the words of a little child,
or upon the wings of an osprey far from the
    treacherous shore.
The Master may come in a single note held long,
or in the thunderous roar of a cascading waterfall.
The Master may arrive unexpectedly with the
    fragrances of fennel or dill.

How the Master will come we cannot say.
That the Master will come we cannot doubt.

The Master lives within you,
has been your companion since before you took
    your first breath of earth's air,
has been with you down all the days of your life,
teaching you, and preparing you against this very day,
calling to you and to you alone,
calling you by your own most intimate name.

When the Master awakens,
he will engage you, and with you
engage the fierce winds of your struggle.
Sunlight will pierce your deepest darkness.

The Master will speak with a voice
so tender, so quiet, and so filled with love.
And you will hear it,
and you will know it,
for it comes from the great Love
of which you yourself are made.

Then you will know calm.
Then you will know strength.
Then you will know peace.

About the Author

Gilbert (Budd) Friend-Jones is an ordained minister in the United Church of Christ who has devoted his life to congregational ministry. A graduate of the Divinity School of Howard University (D. Min.), Princeton Theological Seminary (M. Div.) and Frostburg State University (B.S.), he also is an Oblate of the Order of St. Benedict at St. John's Abbey in Collegeville, MN.

4585082

Made in the USA
Charleston, SC
14 February 2010